OCR

AS

Philosophy and Ethics

OCR and Heinemann are working together to provide better support for you

Ina Taylor

Chris Eyre

Richard Knight

Series Editor: Ina Taylor

www.heinemann.co.uk

✓ Free online support
✓ Useful weblinks
✓ 24 hour online ordering

01865 888080

Official Publisher Partnership

Heinemann is an imprint of Pearson Education Limited, a company incorporated in England and Wales, having its registered office at Edinburgh Gate, Harlow, Essex, CM20 2JE. Registered company number: 872828

www.heinemann.co.uk

Heinemann is a registered trademark of Pearson Education Limited

Text © Ina Taylor 2008

First published 2008

14

10 9

British Library Cataloguing in Publication Data is available from the British Library on request.

ISBN 978 0 435303 62 4

Edited by Beeline Publishing Partnerships Ltd
Typeset by Phoenix Photosetting
Original illustrations © Pearson Education Limited 2008
Cover design by Dickidot Ltd
Picture research by Sally Cole
Cover photo/illustration © Duncan Walker/iStockphoto
Printed in China (CTPS / 09)

The author and publisher would like to thank the following individuals and organisations for permission to reproduce material. Every effort has been made to contact copyright holders of material reproduced in this book. Any omissions will be rectified in subsequent printings if notice is given to the publishers.

Scriptures and additional materials quoted are used with permission from the Good News Bible © 1994 published by the Bible Societies/HarperCollins Publishers Ltd; UK Good News Bible © American Bible Society 1966, 1971, 1976, 1992. News International – p146, 147 (bottom), 156; The Bertrand Russell Peace Organisation – quotations pp50–51; The British Humanist Association – p119; The Guardian – pp 76, 157; The Independent – p147 (top)

Action Press/Rex Features p142; Adrees Latif/Reuters/Corbis p172; Adrian Arbib/Still Pictures p160; AFP/Getty p22; AGStockUSA, Inc./Alamy p55; AKG images p168; Alison Wright/Corbis p114; 1Apix/Alamy p14; The Art Archive/Vatican Museum Rome p19; Bubbles Photolibrary/Alamy p34; Charles Plante Fine Arts/The Bridgeman Art Library p72; Corbis p43; Darren Staples/Reuters/Corbis p74; Don Hammond/Design Pics/Corbis p60; Douglas Pearson/Corbis p45; Dkimages p20; Edward North/Alamy p164; Garry Watson/Science Photo Library p71; Jeremy Sutton Hibbert/Rex Features p162; Jim Naughten/Getty Images p108; John Lawrence/Getty Images p110; Jurgen Reisch/Getty p106; Larry Lefever/Alamy p112; Lawrence Manning/Corbis p99; Makoto Iwafuji/Eurelios/Science Photo Library p158; Malcolm Fairman/Alamy p47; Martin Bedall/Rex Features p31; Museo de Bellas Artes, Seville, Spain/Index/The Bridgeman Art Library p118; Nabil John Elderkin/Getty p95; NASA/JPL-Caltech/Max Plank Institute/Science Photo Library p77, 80; Nora Pelyi/Rex Features p138; Norman Price/Alamy p53; Olaf Doering/Alamy p150; Paul Doyle/Alamy p154; Peter Ryan/Science Photo Library p144; Peter Turnley/Corbis p62; Photodisc Stocktrek p41, 48; Photolibrary.com p148; Private Collection/Archives Charmet/The Bridgeman Art Library p122; Three Graces (marble) by Canova, Antonio (1757–1822) Hermitage, St. Petersburg, Russia/Cameraphoto Arte Venezia/The Bridgeman Art Library p9; Religious Society of Friends p170; Reza/Webistan/Corbis p12; Russell Kightley/Science Photo Library p137; Scott Camazine/Science Photo Library p69; Scott Camazine/Getty Images p140, 156; Sipa Press/Rex Features p124, 152; Steve Gschmeissner/Science Photo Library p83; tbkmedia.de/Alamy p15; Tony Kyriacou/Rex Features p166; Voisin/Phanie/Rex Features p104; William Manning/Corbis p56; Sistine Chapel Ceiling (1508–12): The Creation of Adam, 1511–12 (fresco) (post restoration) by Buonarroti, Michelangelo (1475–1564) Vatican Museums and Galleries, Vatican City, Italy/The Bridgeman Art Library pp29, 32–3

Examination questions, lesson plans and mark schemes are reproduced with permission of OCR.

Contents

Part 2: Religious Ethics

Teacher Introduction

Notes for teachers

This book is designed to support units G571 (AS Philosophy of Religion) and G572 (AS Religious Ethics) of OCR's AS Religious Studies specification first teaching 2008. The specification builds on the knowledge, understanding and skills that candidates may have developed through the study of GCSE Religious Studies or Religious Education. However, the specification does not assume or require any previous study of the subject.

Structure of the book

OCR AS Philosophy and Ethics is divided into six chapters. Chapters 1–4 cover the AS Philosophy of Religion element of the specification (G571) as follows:

▷ Chapter 1: Ancient Greek influences on Philosophy of Religion
▷ Chapter 2: Judaeo-Christian Influences on Philosophy of Religion
▷ Chapter 3: Traditional Arguments for the existence of God
▷ Chapter 4: Challenges to religious belief

Chapters 5 and 6 cover the AS Religious Ethics element of the specification (G572) as follows:

▷ Chapter 5: Ethical theories
▷ Chapter 6: Applied ethics.

The chapters themselves are typically arranged as follows:

▷ Chapter openers – including key terms, learning objectives, and a 'what do you think?' question based on the chapter content.
▷ Content organised by topic in double page spreads, with accompanying activities.
▷ A centre spread linking the main ideas, issues and thinkers covered in the chapter.
▷ An Exam Café section, providing revision tips and exam preparation.

How to use this book

Engagement with, and understanding of, the key philosophical and ethical concepts needs to run throughout teaching and learning for OCR Philosophy and Ethics. *OCR AS Philosophy and Ethics* has been specifically written to provide comprehensive coverage of these concepts, thinkers and movements. The accompanying Activities, For Debate, Making Links, Stretch and Challenge and Taking It Further features are designed to test and consolidate students' understanding and skills.

The content of this book is further supported by extra resources in the Planning and Delivery Resource (PDR) and CD-ROM. These resources vary from worksheets to original extracts from key thinkers to audio, video and PowerPoint resources. Where the content is supported by extra material in the Planning and Development Resources this is indicated on the student book page with the following icon . Similarly, where extra resources are available on the CD-ROM this is signified by the following icon.

Methods of assessment

The AS GCE is made up of two mandatory units chosen from nine options. This book supports two of these nine units: G571 (AS Philosophy of Religion) and G572 (AS Religious Ethics). At AS units are externally assessed and each unit forms 50% of the corresponding four-unit Advanced GCE.

Philosophy of Religion is assessed by a written paper, 1.5 hours for 70 marks. Candidates are required to answer two two-part essay questions from a choice of four.

Religious Ethics is also assessed by a written paper, 1.5 hours for 70 marks. Again, candidates are required to answer two two-part essay questions from a choice of four.

Student introduction

How to use this book

OCR AS Philosophy and Ethics has been specifically written to support you through the study of the OCR AS Philosophy of Religion and AS Religious Ethics units. This book will help you to understand the thinkers, theories and concepts that underlie the topics you are studying. You should refer back to this book during your revision. The Exam Café sections at the end of each chapter will be particularly helpful as you prepare for your exam.

Each chapter in the book makes use of the following features:

Activities

The activities have been designed to help you understand the specification content. They are labelled as AO1 and AO2 according to what type of activity they are and what skills they test.

For Debate

Each chapter will include some For Debate activities, made up of statements, quotes or concepts for you to discuss in pairs, as a group or as a whole class. The For Debate activities have been designed to promote the sharing of ideas, to improve your speaking and listening skills, and also to challenge you to argue from viewpoints that you may not necessarily agree with.

Stretch and Challenge

This feature is designed to stretch your knowledge and understanding. Sometimes this means going beyond the requirements of the specification to further inform your understanding of a concept. Or it could be more probing questions about the topic studied requiring you to think and respond at a higher level.

Making Links

MAKING LINKS AO2 skills

Discuss the way Plato's concept of the Form of the Good might influence the way Christians understand God.

These activities encourage you to make connections between different parts of the course: for example, between different thinkers, concepts and ideas. This will help broaden your understanding of philosophy and ethics by identifying the influences, similarities and differences between different topics.

Further research

FURTHER RESEARCH

Watch the film *The Matrix* (1999). Can you see any links to Plato's Analogy of the Cave?

These contain ideas for further research into particular topics. Completing the Taking It Further activities will extend your knowledge of the specification content.

Key words

KEY WORD

The Greek word **telos**: purpose. An argument concerned with the purpose, or ultimate goal, of something is called a teleological argument.

Definitions of new words can be found in the margin next to where the word appears in the text to help put the word in context.

Exam Café

The Exam Café is the ideal place to be if you are revising content, practising exam questions or if you need some advice about how to be successful in AS Religious Studies.

Here you'll find lots of ideas to help you prepare for your exams. So **Relax**, because there's handy advice from fellow students, **Refresh** yourself with summaries of the key ideas, and Get That **Result** with lots of hints and tips direct from the examiners.

This resource uses the Good News Version of the Bible for quotations from the Bible. Any OCR AS examination questions containing quotations from the Bible will use the New Revised Standard Version of the Bible, but students can quote any version in their exam answers.

Ancient Greek influences on Philosophy of Religion

Is it better to **question** the world around you or to accept what you know to be true? How do **you** know what is true?

In this chapter you will learn:

■ about the thinking of Plato and Aristotle and be able to highlight strengths and weaknesses in their thinking

■ what might be represented in Plato's Analogy of the Cave by the prisoners, the shadows, the cave itself, the outside world, the sun, the journey out of the cave and the return to the prisoners

■ what Plato meant by Forms and demonstrate the relation between concepts and phenomena, the concept of Ideals, the relation between the Form of the Good and the other Forms

■ Aristotle's ideas about cause and purpose in relation to God, his understanding of material, efficient, formal and final cause and the concept of the Prime Mover.

Is it better to **question** the world around you or to accept what you know to be true? How do **you** know what is true?

Ancient Greek influences on Philosophy of Religion

1.1 Plato's Cave

In this topic you will learn what the Greek philosopher Plato thought about reality, illusion and the role of the philosopher in the world.

▌ These are normal people watching an extended edition of Neighbours. What idea of real life would you get if you watched nothing but soaps?

Virtual reality

We are used to virtual reality, things which have the appearance of truth but are not real. Computer games, cyber space, videos and television programmes mean that it is easy to spend your time in an imaginary world. An obsession with celebrities' lives also makes it easy to get caught up watching someone else's lives and loves, to the exclusion of enjoying your own.

In the cartoon above the people sitting on the sofa are completely absorbed in the fictional exploits of the characters in a soap. Apart from eating fast food (packed full of artificial ingredients you'll notice!) they do nothing, not even interact with each other.

Outside their window are the real neighbours, but the TV viewers are totally unaware of them. If one couch potato does make the effort to heave herself up from the sofa and go outside, what will she see? Do you think she will realise how much more interesting it is to socialise with real people?

Let's assume that after a stimulating encounter with her real-life neighbours, the girl returns to the darkened lounge where her friends remain totally engrossed in the soap. What sort of reception would she get?

 ACTIVITY

Role play a conversation between the person returning from outside and the group watching the soap.

Why might the girl who returns say 'Get a life!' to her mates watching Neighbours on television?

 STRETCH & CHALLENGE

What do you think Plato is saying about the value of a philosopher in society?

In the cave

The ancient Greek philosopher Plato (c.428–347 BCE) used a similar analogy to the one in the cartoon. His story was in a setting more familiar to his audience two and a half thousand years ago. The enclosed world he chose was a cave. A group of people are sitting deep in the cave facing the back wall. They have been here since childhood and are chained to prevent them ever looking round to see anything.

Plato continues his story

> *Above and behind them a fire is blazing at a distance, and between the fire and the prisoners there is a raised way; and you will see, if you look, a low wall built along the way, like the screen which marionette-players have in front of them, over which they show the puppets… men were passing along the wall carrying all sorts of vessels, and statues and figures of animals made of wood and stone and various materials, which appear over the wall. Some of them are talking and others silent.*

He goes on to say that because of the position of the fire, the shadows of passers-by appear on the back wall of the cave. The prisoners who sit facing this wall have spent their lives watching this shadow play. For them the appearance seems real because they have never seen anything else.

Eventually one prisoner, who has spent a lifetime chained to the floor, breaks free and makes the slow painful journey out of the cave to the outside world. The first thing he encounters is the sun. After the dim cave, the sun's strength is blinding and his eyes hurt but gradually he gets used to it and can see a colourful world around him. Later he looks up in the sky and sees the sun itself which he realises is the source of life. He begins to work out that the objects of the upper world represent the Forms and the cave was merely a pale shadow form of the reality. In other words, the material world of appearances is a poor copy of the realm of the Forms (see pages 14–16).

He returns to the prisoners to tell them the truth about life but they think he is stupid and carry on watching the shadows on the cave wall.

What is the big idea?

Plato used the cave story to explain the importance of questioning everything like a philosopher does in order to distinguish between the unreal physical world (where firelight casts flickering shadows on a cave wall) and the real spiritual world lit by the sun. The prisoners in the cave are people who just accept everything at face value and never ask questions or try to understand. Their lives are empty and meaningless. The shadows aren't real objects. The one who breaks away and makes the journey out of the cave is the philosopher who wants to know what is really going on. In the outside world he discovers the sun, which he realises is giving life to everything: the sun represents the Form of the Good (see page 16). When the person returns to the cave, he knows life inside is just a sham. The images on the cave wall lack colour. Nothing is clear or sharp. The sounds they hear are muffled and echo. The other prisoners, lacking the philosopher's enquiring mind, continue to live in a dark dismal world.

ACTIVITY
A01 skills

Draw a strip cartoon, or diagram, to illustrate Plato's analogy.

Label the cave/the prisoners/the shadows/the outside world/the sun/the person making the journey out of the cave/the return to the prisoners.

Write a sentence explaining what each point you have labelled represents.

FOR DEBATE
A02 skills

Why is it significant that the shadows the cave dwellers see are of animal statues made from wood and stone?

FURTHER RESEARCH

Watch the film *The Matrix* (1999). Can you see any links to Plato's Analogy of the Cave?

STRETCH & CHALLENGE
A01 skills

Find out how the upper realm in Plato's allegory related to mathematical reasoning. Investigate the Simile of the Divided Line and report to the rest of the class.

1.2 What's in the cave analogy?

In this topic you will examine Plato's ideas in more detail before weighing them up.

FOR DEBATE A02 skills

FOR DEBATE A02 skills

'People who become obsessed by making money lose their grip on reality.' Discuss whether this is really true and what connection this debate might have with Plato's cave.

ACTIVITY A01 skills

Write the released prisoner's blog.

Points to include:

- his fears as he reaches the cave entrance
- the pain and difficulties he experiences with his eyes
- his initial observations and thoughts
- his conclusion a few days later about the sun's effect on life
- the reason he decides to return to the cave
- and his reaction to the return.

KEY WORD

Empirical knowledge is knowledge gained from the senses. **A priori knowledge** is gained from logical reasoning, wholly independent of sense experience.

▌ These Javanese puppeteers entertain their audience to a shadow play. Those watching the performance are like Plato's cave dwellers observing the antics of shadows projected on to a wall. They are fascinated by the illusion. The reality of people carrying little wooden models is not seen.

The seemingly straightforward fable of the cave is actually packed full of meaning and rewards closer examination. Re-acquaint yourself with the story and examine it from a different angle by completing the activity on the left.

Plato was using this story to raise various issues.

What is real?

Everyone in the story is convinced what they are looking at is real. The prisoners' knowledge is based exclusively on their sense of sight and sound and they accept it without question. Plato's story is showing us that their **empirical knowledge** (which is gained from the senses) is flawed. It is not showing them reality. Appearances are deceptive. By contrast the prisoner has discovered reality. After emerging into the real world outside the cave, his power of reasoning leads him to a philosophical understanding of the truth. This **a priori knowledge** of the reality is based totally on reasoning and not on the experience of his senses. Plato is pointing out the need to distinguish between the two realms of appearance and reality, although it is important to note that the simile of the upper world is a metaphor for the Forms and does not represent objects in the material sense (see pages 14–15 for more about the Forms).

How is truth known?

The only person who succeeds in discovering the truth is the prisoner who escapes from the cave. He is prepared to make the long, difficult journey up to the mouth of the cave to reach the real world. It is no accident that the journey is uphill. You can think of lots of imagery to do with travelling upwards and moving from darkness into light. What Plato is saying is that only those escaping the artificial world of the senses, containing shadows, echoes and guesswork, can know the truth. Outside the cave, the prisoner discovers the real objects whose shadows and echoes had formerly entertained him; these are the truth. This leads us on to the Forms (see pages 14–15).

How should society be organised?

The cave represents a world where everyone is held back because they rely on sensory experiences. Our senses are like the flickering shadows on the wall, they are always changing. Although, like the prisoners, we try to understand what our senses tell us, it is futile. The best person to lead a society is the one who can break free of all this; the philosopher. By rejecting sensory experiences, he is open to reality and can apply his intellect to understanding the real world.

Equally worrying in the cave analogy is the fact that when the released prisoner returns to help his fellow inmates, they reject him. They prefer ignorance. Some even want to kill him. Plato undoubtedly had in mind the fate of his own teacher, the philosopher Socrates, who had challenged the ideas of his day and was condemned to death.

Who is the best leader?

In Plato's ideal world, society is led by the philosopher who has no distractions such as a family or material possessions to divert them from the correct way forward.

Will the argument stand up?

Plato's argument is **absolutist**. Absolutist means it is fixed. He believed it to be true for all people in all places and for all time, in other words universal.

Those who criticise Plato's analogy point to the fact that there is no concrete proof that either the world in the cave or outside is real. Everybody in the story is convinced they are living in the true world. How can you prove who is right and who is wrong? Have you ever woken up from a dream that was so vivid that for a while you weren't sure whether any of it had actually happened?

In his book *Nicomachean Ethics*, Aristotle was critical of Plato's argument because he could not agree that the form of something has a separate existence over and above the particular. Other critics have pointed out the elitism of the cave and the rejection of the *a posteriori*. Plato's experience of democracy was very different from our modern representative democracies. So the main point of the allegory, that philosophers are best placed to rule since they have greater knowledge, may overlook the practical skills needed for ruling, by a reliance on an intellectualist approach.

STRETCH & CHALLENGE A01+A02 Skills

Look at Plato's original story to find out what sort of games the prisoners in the cave played. Would you criticise them as games? What would the philosopher say about the games?

FOR DEBATE A02 skills

If the cave dwellers are happy in their ignorance, it is better to leave them to it.

KEY WORD

Absolute means a truth which never varies.

ACTIVITY 1.1

- Draw a spider diagram with the cave in the middle and display as many strands of meaning as you can. A01 skills
- Build up a list of strengths and weaknesses in the analogy of Plato's cave. A01 skills

Ancient Greek influences on Philosophy of Religion

1.3 Plato's got Form

In this topic you will examine in detail Plato's beliefs that the world we live in is not the real one.

❚ Do you think this person's activity has any value? Why? For whom?

ACTIVITY   A01 skills

Script, or role play, a chat show interview between Plato and an award winning artist whose work has given lots of people pleasure.

Searching for reality

Plato would have had scant regard for the artist in the photograph. Whilst agreeing the painter had recognised something beautiful in the scene in front of him, Plato would say he is wasting his time producing a pale imitation of that beauty. Plato rejected art, which is a product of the senses, preferring instead mathematics, which is an expression of pure thought that can explain a pure form. (Remember the cave dwellers who relied on their senses to interpret the world?)

The artist and his painting is a useful concept to think around because it helps us understand some of Plato's ideas about the world we inhabit. Let's take the artist. He is looking at the scene in front of him and recognises that it is beautiful. Most people would agree with him. In fact it is hard to imagine anyone would disagree. Some may know of more beautiful places and others might point out there are parts of this landscape that could be better. Nevertheless, no matter what nationality or culture we are, we would all recognise there is some beauty in this scene.

It is hard to define beauty but we all know it when we see it. This led Plato to say that there is indeed a Form (which he gives a capital F to) called beauty which we have a dim recollection of from our prior existence in the realm of the Forms. When we see something that contains elements of this Form we recognise it as beautiful.

Where does this Form exist?

According to Plato the world we live in is a pale imitation of the real world. (Once again you will recognise the analogy of the cave and the outside world.) Our world is constantly changing and we rely on our senses to understand what is going on. You are not the same person you were three years ago, indeed you are not the same person you were three hours ago – even three minutes ago! Cells are forever changing and ideas flit through our minds like monkeys swinging through trees. Plato was sure the real world is outside the one we live in. This real world is unchanging and eternal. It is the world of ideas not of senses, where there are perfect forms of the things we know on earth.

Plato's world of forms contains fixed truths which are absolutely true for *all* time, people and place.

The Particulars participate in the Form

You have probably decided that four legs, two ears and a tail make a dog. Somebody might quite rightly have pointed out that a horse has that too and some dogs have a docked tail. Start again! It can seem impossible to get a clear definition to cover the essence of a dog yet rule out other animals, but a three-year-old has no difficulty distinguishing a dog from another animal. The child is identifying the Form whilst we are getting bogged down with the details. Does a dog need pointed ears or floppy ones, a long coat or a short hair and so on? The Form is not a shape, it is the essence of an object, in this case a dog and all dogs have a degree of 'dogginess' due to participating in the Form. It is this From a child recognises. The Particular, on the other hand, is concerned with the superficial details that over-lay that Form.

Recognising Forms

Plato said we recognise the Forms because we are born with a dim recollection of them from our prior existence in the realm of the Forms. There is an inner part of us, you might call it the soul, that does not change. It is eternal and, before it became tied down by a body, it was connected with the real world of Forms. It is because we have all seen the Forms before, that we can recognise them now.

ACTIVITY A01 skills

Which one is a dog? This may seem a silly question because although they look different, we know they are both dogs. Write down the essential qualities that define a dog.

ACTIVITY A01 skills

Explain why Plato says the world we live in is not the real world.

STRETCH & CHALLENGE A02 skills

What would you say to challenge the idea that the recognition of Form proves we have an eternal soul?

How do you explain the fact that everyone can identify something such as kindness?

ACTIVITY A01 skills

Cut out a photograph of a pair of trousers and stick it on a page. Sketch out an ideas map that considers your factual knowledge of the trousers and your opinion of them. Circle the a priori information in red and circle the empirical information in green. Which information is the most useful?

Ancient Greek influences on Philosophy of Religion

1.4 The Form of the Good

In this topic you will consider where the argument about Plato's Forms takes us and what its strengths and weaknesses are.

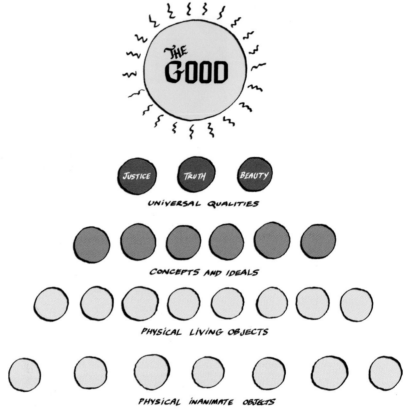

Plato's Form of the Good

Plato believed most things conform to a Form, but some things like number and evil do not. He also thought that some Forms are greater than others. Ideal Forms have something in common, which is that they all have the presence of Good in them. For that reason, Plato said, the Good is the most important Form, it is 'the Form of the Forms'. (You might find it easier to think of this as the ideal of these ideal forms.)

Remember the story of the cave? In the outside world where reality dwelt, one Form was stronger than the others. The sun. The prisoner relied on light from the sun to recognise the other forms in the real world. This is Plato's analogy for the Good. Once you can understand Good, it will enable you to understand other Forms such as Justice and Beauty because they are all aspects of goodness. The Good illuminates everything else, the further away from the Good you get, the paler things become.

ACTIVITY A01 skills

Try and explain the concept of Justice without referring to the concept of Good in any way. This means you can't use a word like 'fairness' without implying that it relates to what is good.

16

According to Plato, knowledge of the Good is the highest knowledge a human is capable of. The ordinary person struggles to see past the illusion of this world because they are ruled by their senses. It is like the ordinary person who watches the conjurer and accepts her trick at face value. Only the person who investigates and questions learns the truth behind the illusion. Only the philosopher is capable of seeing beyond, because he can make a priori judgements. Because he thinks independently of the senses in his search for Truth, he can see into the world of the Forms where Good is.

What are the strengths and weaknesses of Plato's Forms?

STRENGTHS

It explains why we all recognise the same essential elements in something.

This argument helps us to understand why there are imperfections in the world around us.

It encourages us to question in order to learn and not to accept things at face value.

WEAKNESSES

You can't prove Plato's 'real' world of the Forms actually exists.

If you can have a Form of a Form (like Goodness) what's stopping you having a form of a form of a form of … (This argument is called **infinite regression** because it goes on forever backwards). Some people say there is no such absolute value as Good. It is all shades of opinion; it is subjective, which means people will have their own opinion about what is good. This makes it less likely that two people will always come to the same conclusion about what is good.

It seems unlikely that everything in existence has an ideal form. Could you have an ideal slug or type of cancer for instance?

Plato's argument is no help for making sense of the world we live in.

Plato believes the senses are inferior, yet humans have relied on them for survival for thousands of years.

Plato is not clear how the world of Forms relates to our world. Does the dog Form have to relate to a specific variety of dog? Is there a distinct Form of Greyhound? And within that could there be a distinct Form of male Greyhound and white three-legged varieties? And so it goes on…

Ancient Greek influences on Philosophy of Religion

1.5 Mr Plato, meet Mr Aristotle

In this topic you will think about how Raphael's painting 'The School of Athens' contains useful clues about the way these two philosophers approached their search for meaning.

The background

Plato, who as a young man had studied under the philosopher Socrates, went on to found his own academy in Athens in 387 BCE. This Athenian centre of learning advanced European knowledge in a wide range of subjects such as maths, science, politics and astronomy as well as philosophy.

In 367 BCE when Plato was sixty, seventeen-year-old Aristotle arrived at the Academy as a student. He studied there for twenty years and was recognised as a brilliant student.

Raphael's painting, executed in 1514, is obviously an imaginary view of life at the Academy of Athens. What interests us are the central figures of Plato and Aristotle, but everyone of note is also depicted in this picture. Heraclitus, who wondered whether you could step in the same river twice, sits to the left of centre.

Which of the two central figures must be Plato?

He points upwards. How can you link that with his philosophy of Forms?

Look at his feet. They appear to be about to move, which is significant. Remember him saying the problem with our world of the senses is that everything is constantly changing? In his hand he holds a copy of one of his great works 'Timaeus'. Notice how he is holding the book; once again he is pointing upwards.

Now compare these same features – hands, feet and book – with those of Aristotle for clues to the difference between these philosophers' approaches. Although Aristotle had great affection and respect for his teacher, he disagreed with him. Aristotle was an empiricist, who argued that knowledge is based on experience and the truth can be arrived at through our senses. This explains why his hand and his book on 'Ethics' are both held parallel to the ground. The answers lie in the physical world. His feet are firmly on the ground and completely still, in contrast to Plato's.

Ancient Greek influences on Philosophy of Religion

1.6 What's the cause of this?

In this topic you will consider Aristotle's ideas about what causes something to exist and the four parts of those causes.

What's in the picture?

This is not a trick question. Aristotle (384–322 BCE), like other philosophers, was trying to understand the purpose of life. One area he examined involved trying to discover exactly what the essence of an object was. In contrast to his teacher, Aristotle began with the world around him, the world of experience and senses, in order to reason why anything exists at all. This means Aristotle would have looked at a real table and thought about it, rather than use Plato's approach of looking beyond the object to the theoretical ideal Form of a table that might exist in another world.

Aristotle concluded there were four causes for the existence of an object. Let's consider them in relation to this everyday piece of furniture.

What material is this made of?

This table is made of wood and glue and nails. Aristotle called this stage the Material Cause. Materials always have the **potential** for change. You have only got to think what would happen if the table was left outside for years in all weathers or if it caught fire. The materials represent the impermanence of our world. The important question for this cause is: *What's it made of?*

How was it made?

This table happened because a person chose to manufacture it. This stage is the Efficient Cause and the important the question here is: *How does it happen?* Don't forget that an Efficient Cause may not be a person. A gust of wind may be the Efficient Cause of a tree falling over. Just as with a cake, the efficient cause is not only the baker, but the mixing and cooking process.

What are the characteristics of a table?

We recognise this as a table because it has four legs and a flat surface on the top and it belongs to a group we call 'furniture'. What we are doing is looking at the design of the object then mentally fitting it into a category we already know. This is the Formal Cause. The important question here is: *What are its characteristics?*

What is it for?

A table provides us with a useful surface to put things on. Here Aristotle examines the purpose of the object, the reason it exists at all. He called it the Final Cause. The important question here is: *What's it for?*

The really important question

Aristotle said this fourth question was the really important one because it gave the best explanation of an object. We can identify with that. If someone shows you an electronic gadget they have bought you may well be interested. But it won't be long before you ask, 'What's it for?' If the answer is 'nothing', then your interest will immediately cease. No matter how intriguing the object looks, if it doesn't do anything, what's the point? We have to satisfy ourselves that something has a purpose for it to be worthy of our attention. Aristotle is effectively saying the same thing. The purpose of an object is an important part of what it is.

Aristotle said everything in existence can answer those four causes, but it is worth remembering that we may not actually know the answers ourselves. That is why people have found it hard to know what purpose a slug or a disease such as cancer serve. You could argue that the purpose of a cancerous cell is to replicate itself as quickly as possible. If it succeeds it has achieved its final cause. If a small object such as a bacterium can answer all the questions, so can something as large as the universe. Where can that lead us?

That's perfect

If the electronic gadget actually works extremely well doing whatever it was sold for, that's perfect. As Aristotle put it, when the purpose is fully realised then full perfection is reached. If the object does what it is meant to do, then the object has achieved goodness, according to Aristotle. Clearly he is using the word 'goodness' in a way we might not have expected. Or is he?

The cancer that spread furiously realised its purpose and, according to Aristotle's definition, achieved perfection. The problem for us is that we have a narrow focus when it comes to things like cancer. We only see illness and pain. According to Aristotle everything has a purpose, even if we do not understand it.

Ancient Greek influences on Philosophy of Religion

1.7 Prime Mover

In this topic you will investigate what Aristotle means by the Prime Mover and consider how Christians might apply this idea.

> *The series must start with something, since nothing can come from nothing.'*
> Aristotle, *Metaphysics*

Like Plato, Aristotle recognised that everything in life is changing; people grow old, day turns to night, tides ebb and flow and so on. Aristotle reasoned that something was causing this movement: he called that being the Prime Mover. The domino image is helpful to some extent in understanding Aristotle's thought.

▌ This was one of the 2006 world record attempts for domino toppling. Millions of dominoes went down — but someone had to push the first one over. Only when the last domino has fallen will the whole picture be revealed from above. Each domino falling on the next knows nothing of the picture.

The Prime Mover

> *There must be a mover which moves them, without being moved, eternal and a substance and actual.*
> Aristotle, *Metaphysics*

At the start a person has to push the first domino over, then stand back and let events happen. The starter really has to exist (have substance) and stand still whilst they topple the first one (stationary). The starter cannot be another domino because it too would need to be pushed. No, the starter has to be different, separate and external from the domino pattern on the floor.

Does there have to be a Prime Mover?

It is clear from Aristotle's words that he was looking at something far more profound than a row of dominoes. He was looking at the changing nature of life and concluded there must be an explanation for all the changes that happen in the universe. Utilising his argument about Causes, Aristotle reasoned that everything must have a Final Cause, in other words a purpose for being here. Nothing comes from nothing, he said. So it follows that when there is a chain of events, there must be an ultimate cause. The Prime Mover is the Final Cause.

What is the Prime Mover like?

Remember the domino image? The person who started the movement had to be totally outside of, and separate from, the dominoes on the floor.

Aristotle's Prime Mover has to be outside of the universe and outside of time. If not, then you could ask the question, what started the Prime Mover and what happened before it existed? Remember infinite regression (see page 17)?

The Prime Mover has to be eternal and really exist but not in a bodily form like us otherwise it would be subject to change just as we are. Aristotle's Prime Mover can only exist in a spiritual way, it must be intelligence or thought.

God and the Prime Mover

You can see there are some similarities between Aristotle's Prime Mover and God, indeed people have referred to the Prime Mover as God.

Aristotle's God is eternal, which he defines as not being dependent on anything else for its existence. It never changes, does not have any potential to change and so will never end. The Prime Mover is actual, something which never changes, is not made of a material. Aristotle's God is immaterial, so can only undertake intellectual and spiritual activities.

For Aristotle something which is eternal must necessarily be good; things which change are bad. Change means impermanence, that is bad because there is always room for improvement. Although the Prime Mover cannot move, things are attracted to it. We humans move towards the Prime Mover, like moths drawn to a light. That is all we can do.

Because Aristotle's God is perfection, it can't think about anything but itself. That is because thinking involves moving through ideas and Aristotle's being is unmoved, so God can only know God. God cannot have any relationship with anything outside of itself. God is 'the thought of thought'. This God is totally outside of our world in terms of time and space. It knows nothing about it, has no plan for it and never intervenes in it.

Weaknesses in the argument

It is hard to understand how the Prime Mover can be powerful, yet be unable to know it.

If the Prime Mover is eternal thought, where did the matter that the world is made of come from? Was it caused, too?

Does there have to be a reason, or final cause, for the existence of the universe? Couldn't it be chance?

ACTIVITY A01 skills

The domino image is really an example of an efficient cause, not a final cause. Explain why, and how, the domino analogy could be misleading when considering Aristotle's Prime Mover.

STRETCH & CHALLENGE

In pairs evaluate Aristotle's ideas on Causes or the Prime Mover. Report your thoughts back to the whole group.

A02 skills

FOR DEBATE A02 skills

Aristotle's Prime Mover is completely different to the Christian concept of God.

Exam Café
Relax, refresh, result!

Relax and prepare

What I wish I'd known at the start of the year...

Charmaine

Being at college was great. I found that we had a lot of free time. Me and my mates would go shopping in our free periods. Sometimes we would miss our bus back from town and I missed RS a few times. The teachers at college are really understanding; they treat you as adults and don't hassle you if you miss the odd class. A couple of weeks before the exam we were revising in class and I noticed that Rachel's folder was twice the size of mine. It was all the work that I was away for. It's not really my fault, no one told me to copy up. She also had some notes from a revision website. I began to panic and decided to avoid RS for the rest of the week.

Nadia

When people said that AS was harder than GCSE, I guess I didn't really believe them. Most things in class were OK. I didn't do much work outside of lessons. When I came to revise a couple of days before the exams, I found that I couldn't remember half the stuff. So on the day of the exam I went into college an hour early to get help from my teacher – but she wasn't there. I had stopped writing before the half way point of the exam: not a good sign.

Although names and a few details have been changed, unfortunately Nadia, Charmaine and Joseph's stories are all true to life. How can you learn from their mistakes as you prepare for *your* AS year? What do you need to do differently?

Joseph

My teacher said something about not being organised; I wasn't really sure what he meant and was afraid to ask. I had my own system of taking a folder to school every day which I used for all my subjects. When it got full, I emptied it (a pile on my bedroom floor to be precise) and started again. I did this four times during the year. I never got round to sorting it out. To make things worse I tripped over it after a very good night out. I was carrying a cup of coffee at the time. All the notes were ruined.

Getting started...

What's so different about AS?

It is harder than GCSE: You might find yourself tempted to put in minimal effort, particularly if you did OK in your GCSEs without doing any real revision. That would be a mistake!

It is not a memory test: Whilst it is true that you will need to remember a lot of information, the exams are testing whether you can apply the relevant information in answering the question.

It requires longer answers: The questions are of an essay style and although you could give quite brief answers to some of them, you will not fully answer the question (and hence not get good marks) unless you give an extended, detailed response.

Refresh your memory

Revision checklist for Plato and Aristotle

In order to do well on this area of the course you will need to:

▷ Understand what Plato means in his analogy of the cave and be able to explain his symbolism: i.e. prisoners, shadows, the cave itself, sun, journey and return to the prisoners.

▷ Assess the points he is making, do they make sense?

▷ Know what Plato means by the idea of 'Forms'.

▷ Understand how these concepts relate to the particulars.

▷ Understand the Form of the Good.

▷ Be able to discuss whether Plato's ideas on the Forms are appealing.

▷ Show knowledge and understanding of Aristotle's four causes (material, efficient, formal and final).

▷ Be able to explain his concept of the Prime Mover.

▷ Assess the ideas of Aristotle; do you think they work?

Remember that in your final AS exam you will be answering two-part questions. Part a) questions are testing your knowledge and understanding of the material that you have studied. Part b) questions are testing your ability to evaluate ideas.

Common mistakes – Plato

▷ Do you know the truth about the cave? Many students have amusing (though the marks they get for them are not funny) and inaccurate ways of describing the cave, possibly as a result of only half listening in class. Why not try reading what Plato actually says in the *Republic* (section 514–521)? Translations are readily available on the internet.

▷ Do you know what Plato means? The exam questions will focus on what Plato meant in the story of the cave. Some students attempt to give a modern slant to Plato, perhaps interpreting the story of the cave in terms of conversion to Christianity. However valid this may be, it is not what Plato meant.

Get the result!

Building a part a) answer

The next two pages give you some examples of model answers on Plato's Cave. Before turning over to look at the sample answers, try constructing your own part a) answer from this essay plan. Each statement corresponds to a paragraph.

Introduction: prisoners in cave, what is represented.

Escaped prisoner, meaning.

Outside world, return to cave.

Summary of the point of the analogy.

How to plan your answer:

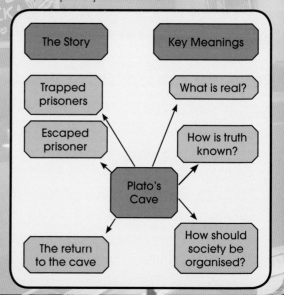

The Story — Key Meanings

Trapped prisoners — What is real?

Escaped prisoner — How is truth known?

Plato's Cave

The return to the cave — How should society be organised?

Sample answers

Exam question

a) Show what ideas Plato is trying to convey in his analogy of the cave. (25 marks)

Sam's original answer

Plato lived from 428-348 BCE. He was a Greek philosopher who was taught by Socrates. Plato in turn taught Aristotle. These were probably the greatest philosophers in Ancient Greece. Plato wrote many books. The most famous of these is 'The Republic'. This book discusses the theme of justice and the idea that society should be ruled by philosophers.

In his story of the cave, Plato asks us to imagine a group of prisoners chained up and only seeing shadows on the wall in front of them. These shadows are produced by a fire.

Examiner says

This is interesting background information on Plato, but is not relevant to the question. The idea that society should be ruled by philosophers cannot be credited as they haven't linked this to the cave.

Examiner says

This is slightly better. The story of the cave is described but the details are not precise. However, crucially, the candidate has failed to show the ideas conveyed by Plato, which is the key aspect of the question.

People on the road make these shadows using objects. They talk to each other and the prisoners think that it is the shadows making the noises. One day a prisoner escapes from the cave. He sees the sun and the objects outside the cave. He goes back to tell the other prisoners what is outside the cave. They don't believe him.

Plato's story has been criticised by some people as there is no evidence that we are living in a Matrix-type world. He can't prove that to be true. The things around us do seem real.

Sam's improved answer

Plato was a philosopher who lived in Ancient Greece. In his book 'The Republic' he sums up his views in the analogy of the cave. Plato describes a cave where prisoners are chained so that they have to face the wall. Behind them is a fire and a road. Shadows cast by objects held by those on the road cause shadows on the wall in front of the prisoners. The prisoners think that these shadows are real things. When noises are heard in the cave, the prisoners assume that the shadows are talking. Plato is representing our condition as human beings; our senses chain us and cause us to accept the world around us, symbolised by the cave. He argues that we are wrong to think that our world is the sum total of reality.

Then one of the prisoners was released. He is dazed and confused. It is a hard journey getting out of the cave. Eventually, when his eyes adjust to the light, he is able to look at real objects in the world outside the cave. Here Plato is representing the philosopher who learns not to trust their senses. The journey to knowledge is difficult and we have to go against our commonsense views. If we do this, Plato thinks that, just like the escaped prisoner, we will be able to see the Forms. The most important Form is the Form of the Good.

The escaped prisoner returns to the cave to tell the others the truth. They do not listen and threaten to kill him if he continues the nonsense about the 'real world'. Plato uses the story of the cave to argue that this world is not as real as the Forms, he argues that it is through philosophy that true knowledge can be obtained; this makes the philosopher the best person to rule society. However, society will be unlikely to appreciate this and may kill the philosopher — this is what happened to his teacher, Socrates.

Examiner says

This whole paragraph is not relevant. Part a) questions are Assessment Objective 1 (AO1); the examiner is testing your knowledge and understanding, not your ability to argue. Overall, the answer shows some knowledge of the topic but is unlikely to reach the higher bands.

Examiner says

A good paragraph, the candidate could have said a little more about the Forms.

Examiner says

A much better answer already. It is detailed and well explained.

Examiner says

A very good answer to the question. A little more detail and explanation of Plato's ideas – such as the Forms, the role of the senses or other relevant areas – would have made this an even better answer.

Are things good because God commands them to be good, or does God command them because they are already good?

In this chapter you will learn:

- about the biblical concept of God as creator and consider the meaning of creatio ex nihilo

- to make a comparison between the idea of Aristotle's Prime Mover and biblical ideas of God

- about the biblical idea of the goodness of God and how it relates to God as law-giver and judge.

Are things good because **God** commands them to be good, or does God command them **because** they are already good?

Judaeo-Christian influences on Philosophy of Religion

2.1 God the Creator

In this topic you will examine the Judaeo-Christian concept of God as the Creator

Ancient Greeks, like Plato and Aristotle, began trying to understand life with philosophical reasoning and arrived at an understanding of a higher being. Jews and Christians would call a higher being God and begin from the standpoint that God exists because the Bible says so. For them the Bible is a sacred text, which contains the words of God. Some believe the words are literally what God said and others believe God inspired humans to write the message down. Either way the Bible is no ordinary book, this is a sacred text which guides believers to a better understanding of God.

God in Genesis

The Bible opens with accounts of God and creation. There are two creation stories in Genesis. That in Genesis 1 is concerned primarily with the creation of the universe whereas the story in Genesis 2 sets out in more detail God's relationship with humanity. Both hold the key to the Judaeo-Christian understanding of God. There are many other writings about God and God's relationship with humanity within the Old and New Testaments, and these also contribute to believers' concept of God. They also show that Jews and Christians believe God has a continuing relationship with his creation.

The concept of creatio ex nihilo

The meaning of this Latin term is much as it appears: creation from nothing. It is the belief that God created the whole universe, along with everything in existence, out of nothing. This was a deliberate action by God and one that is good. It means that God is the master of the world and its contents but that God remains outside of his creation. From your study of Genesis 2 in the Activity on the left, you saw that all parts of creation have an intimate relationship with their creator.

> *In the beginning, when God created the universe, the earth was formless and desolate. The raging ocean that covered everything was engulfed in total darkness, and the power of God was moving over the water.*
>
> Genesis 1:1-2

God the craftsman

▍ The creation of this sculpture required many skills in addition to those of the mason. Someone planned it, designed it on paper, calculated the proportions and weight. The architect incorporated it in the building. There is a purpose to the sculpture. People looking at the sculpture admire the skill of the creator.

In Job 38:4-6 the God who speaks directly to Job is portrayed as the skilled builder of the world.

Were you there when I made the world?

If you know so much, tell me about it.

Who decided how large it would be?

Who stretched the measuring-line over it?

Do you know all the answers?

What holds up the pillars that support the earth?

Who laid the corner-stone of the world?

The creation of humanity

Both Genesis stories show that God regards humans as the highest point of his creation. In Genesis 1, the universe is created piece by piece and finally humanity is placed on the earth to rule it. Genesis 2 contains a briefer account of God's creation of the earth and plant life but it is clear that these were set up ready for God's most important creation, humanity. Although animals are created next, they are made for the benefit of humans.

One very significant difference you will have noticed between the way God is portrayed in the two Genesis stories is God's interaction with humanity. The God in Genesis 2 speaks directly to the humans he created. There is a relationship between God and his creation that enables God to bless people and to punish them. This is very different from the sterile power envisaged by the ancient Greeks.

2.2 What is meant by God?

In this topic you will consider some of the beliefs Jews and Christians have about the nature of God. Some ideas you will have met before, others may be new to you.

ACTIVITY

Which of God's attributes does the artist Michelangelo succeed in showing in this famous painting?

ACTIVITY

Write each key term on a slip of paper. Then write the definitions on other slips of paper. Test yourself by matching the correct terms and definitions.

STRETCH & CHALLENGE

Find out what the sixth century scholar Boethius added to the debate about God.

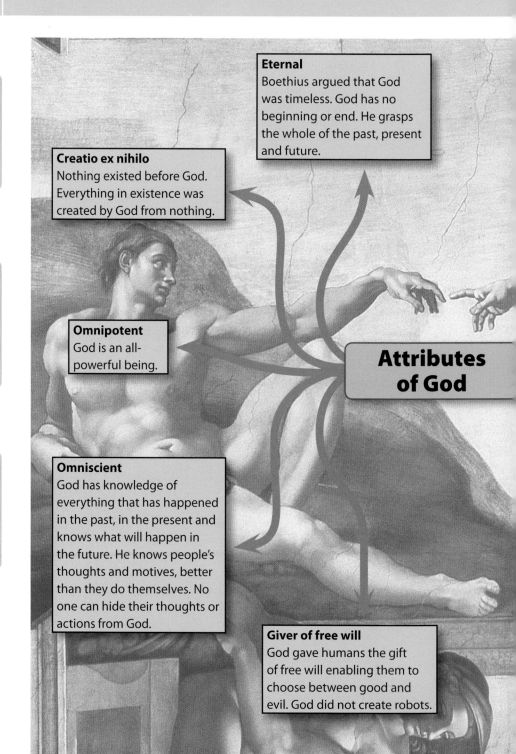

Eternal
Boethius argued that God was timeless. God has no beginning or end. He grasps the whole of the past, present and future.

Creatio ex nihilo
Nothing existed before God. Everything in existence was created by God from nothing.

Omnipotent
God is an all-powerful being.

Attributes of God

Omniscient
God has knowledge of everything that has happened in the past, in the present and knows what will happen in the future. He knows people's thoughts and motives, better than they do themselves. No one can hide their thoughts or actions from God.

Giver of free will
God gave humans the gift of free will enabling them to choose between good and evil. God did not create robots.

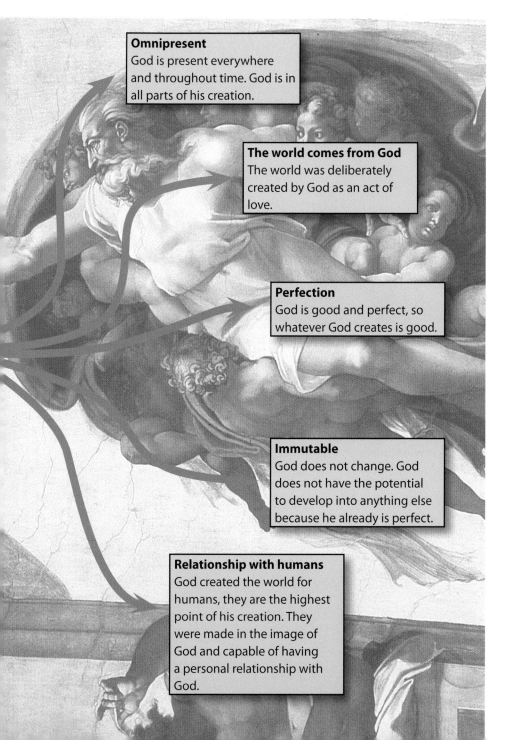

Omnipresent
God is present everywhere and throughout time. God is in all parts of his creation.

The world comes from God
The world was deliberately created by God as an act of love.

Perfection
God is good and perfect, so whatever God creates is good.

Immutable
God does not change. God does not have the potential to develop into anything else because he already is perfect.

Relationship with humans
God created the world for humans, they are the highest point of his creation. They were made in the image of God and capable of having a personal relationship with God.

ACTIVITY

A01 skills

Create your own spider diagrams to show Plato's concept of Good and Aristotle's concept of the Prime Mover. You may be able to link the two diagrams to form a God of the Ancient Greek Philosophers with various legs coming from the centre or you may prefer to keep it as two separate diagrams. Begin by looking at each of the concepts used on this page to see whether any are applicable. Even if the name is the same, like Eternal, be careful to check whether the ideas are exactly the same or not. Then return to the work you did on Plato and Aristotle to see if there are any other concepts you should include.

FOR DEBATE

A02 skills

'If God created everything, He is responsible for everything.'

In your discussions, consider issues such as evil, free will and evolution.

At the end of the debate write a couple of paragraphs summarising the points raised in discussion.

Judaeo-Christian influences on Philosophy of Religion

2.3 God is good

In this topic you will examine the belief in the goodness of God and consider the implications of this belief.

From studying the Bible, a scholar gets many different ideas about the attributes of God. The Old Testament, which is also the Hebrew Bible of the Jews, portrays different aspects of God from those which appear in the Christian New Testament. Nevertheless what underpins both scriptures is the idea of a God who is good.

ACTIVITY A01+A02 Skills

Look back to your definitions of what made certain things good on pages 16–17 in this book. Continuing from that, decide what you think makes a good person? What makes a good parent? What does it mean to say God is good?

The love of a parent for their child is one that most people can understand. It is a love that does not mean giving them everything they want or letting them do what they like. Explain why this is?

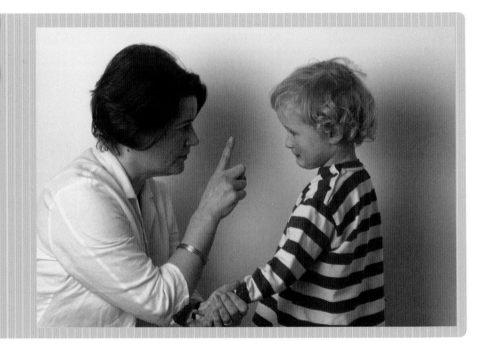

ACTIVITY A01 skills

Analyse Hannah's story, which comes from the Old Testament, and extract as many points as you can about the nature of God and his goodness.

The Bible has many accounts of God's goodness towards humanity. Here is one woman's personal encounter with God.

Hannah, the wife of Elkanah, was upset because she had no children so she prayed to God.

> *Hannah made a solemn promise: "Almighty Lord, look at me, your servant! See my trouble and remember me! Don't forget me! If you give me a son, I promise that I will dedicate him to you, for his whole life, and that he will never have his hair cut." Hannah continued to pray to the Lord for a long time … and the Lord answered her prayer. So it was that she became pregnant, and gave birth to a son. She named him Samuel, and explained, "I asked the Lord for him."*
> 1 Samuel 1: 10–11 and 20

Why is God morally perfect?

Christians and Jews believe God is perfect because the Bible states he is. They find evidence to support this in the world he created. For them, perfection and goodness are the same when speaking of God. God is the source of all goodness in the world and this goodness filters down through all his creation. For Christians especially, God's goodness equates to love, and they regard the creation of the world as an act of love.

God the good law-giver and judge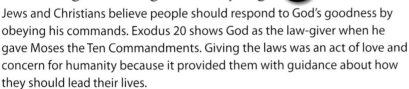

Jews and Christians believe people should respond to God's goodness by obeying his commands. Exodus 20 shows God as the law-giver when he gave Moses the Ten Commandments. Giving the laws was an act of love and concern for humanity because it provided them with guidance about how they should lead their lives.

It follows therefore that, like the concerned parent, God is full of righteous anger, often called righteous indignation, if his people do not obey his commands. In some of the quotations you read, there is evidence that God responds with anger and punishment if people disobey him. In the same way, a parent who doesn't care if their child breaks the rules at home or in the street would hardly be considered a good, loving parent. A good God punishes wrong-doers so they can learn from their mistakes.

The Christian view of God's goodness

For Christians, God's goodness is seen in the person of Jesus, whom they believe was the Son of God. Read the explanation in John's Gospel.

> *For God loved the world so much that he gave his only Son, so that everyone who believes in him may not die but have eternal life. For God did not send his Son into the World to be its judge, but to be its saviour.*

This concept of God shows him to be very much a part of his creation and inter-acting as a human, through the person of Jesus, with the humans he created. Christians regard the teachings and actions of Jesus as further examples of God's goodness. That God was prepared to let his son, Jesus, die for humanity, is seen by Christians as further proof of his goodness.

In the Old Testament book of Job, a good man suffers one disaster after another. Throughout it all, Job remains faithful and obedient to God even though he cannot understand the undeserved calamities. Ultimately his unquestioning faith in God is rewarded. Questioning and reasoning are not needed.

God's goodness lacks nothing. It cannot be improved upon; it is not potential but actual.

STRETCH & CHALLENGE

Choose further examples to extract evidence of God's goodness.

Luke 1: 46–55

Psalm 18: 20–27

Jeremiah 15:6–9

Exodus 20.

ACTIVITY

Explain how this God is different to Aristotle's Prime Mover.

ACTIVITY

What does the extract from John's Gospel say about God's love?

FOR DEBATE

Does God command things because they are good, or are things good because God commands them?

Plato posed a similar question when he asked, 'Do the gods love what is good because it is good? Or is something good because the gods love it?'

Decide what the difference is. Then try to decide what a Christian might say.

Exam Café
Relax, refresh, result!

Relax and prepare

Tim

I thought this area would be easy as I have been going to church for much of my life. I soon realised that knowing what my pastor says about these texts was not enough. The AS requires an academic study of the text. It was interesting to find out what ideas there are about the Biblical stories of creation.

Ibrar

This topic seemed quite easy at first. So I was surprised and disappointed to get a low mark on the practice question we did in class. My teacher went through it with me and I learned that the focus of the question was on how the writers 'explain'. I had just described what the stories said.

Bryn

I had to sort of forget what I learned at GCSE where you could get most of the marks by just listing a couple of arguments for, a couple against and saying what you think. You have to argue both sides still, but in a lot more detail.

Getting started. . .

Remember that in your final AS exam you will be answering two-part questions.

Part a) questions are testing your knowledge and understanding of the material that you have studied.

Part b) questions are testing your ability to evaluate ideas.

Gulshan

I found learning the technique of writing an argument really useful. I used to do well in class discussion but wonder why my written work was not as good. My teacher explained that I was leaving gaps in my arguments.

Refresh your memory

Revision checklist for the Judeo-Christian influences on Philosophy of Religion

In order to do well on this area of the course you will need to:

▷ Be able to explain how the Bible shows God to be a creator.

▷ Understand the creation stories in Genesis 1 and 2, but you do not have to limit yourselves to these.

▷ Consider the idea of God as craftsman.

▷ Know what creatio ex nihilo means and consider whether this idea is Biblical.

▷ Be able to define and explain omnipotence, omniscience and omnipresence in relation to God.

▷ Make comparisons between the Biblical ideas of God and Aristotle's Prime Mover.

▷ Assess whether the idea of God as creator means that God is responsible for everything that happens in the universe.

▷ Explain what the Bible means in stating that God is good.

▷ Be able to explain God's goodness by referring to the ideas of law-giver, judge and God as being morally perfect.

▷ Assess whether God causes things to be good by giving commands or whether God commands things that are already good. (This is called the Euthyphro Dilemma.)

Examiner's tips

▷ **Some candidates** assume that their Biblical knowledge, perhaps from Sunday school or primary school RE, will be adequate. It is important to ensure that you explain rather than describe.

▷ **The key lesson** is to prepare for this with the same rigour that you would when studying the Greeks – material that you are completely unfamiliar with.

▷ **It is important to make sure that you are specific**. In giving a detailed response, use evidence from the texts to make conclusions rather than just indulging in storytelling.

Get the result!

Sample answers

Exam question

(a) How do the writers of the Bible explain the concept of God as creator? (25 marks)

Extract from Ibrar's answer

The Bible describes the creation of the world in Genesis chapter 1. Here we see God creating the world in seven days. On the first day God says 'let there be light' and light appears. On the second day God separates the sky and the sea. On the third day, God commands trees and plants and they appear. The fourth day sees God creating the sun, the moon and the stars. God made the sun to rule the day and the moon and stars to rule the night. On the fifth day God starts to make living creatures. He makes the fish and the birds. The sixth day sees God creating all the animals and then human beings in his own image. On the seventh day God rested.

Modern thinkers doubt whether this story really happened. They use Darwin's theory of evolution to say that the Bible was just made up and the story isn't true. Christians reject this as this would mean that the story has no value. However Darwin's theory is just a theory and although there is some scientific evidence for it, it is not proven. So the idea that God is creator is not really challenged by these thinkers.

Examiner says

Ibrar has made a common mistake. He has answered this 'explain' type question as if it were a 'describe' question. His first sentence shows that he has not really understood what the question wanted him to do. His teacher will have explained to him that there needs to be a theological explanation of how the Bible presents God as creator rather than a description of how God is said to create.

Examiner says

Ibrar has made what is quite a common mistake. He has included argument in his part a) answer. He won't lose marks for this but he won't gain any either because it is not what the question asks for. He is not explaining 'how the writers explain the concept of God as creator.' The third sentence indicates a lack of understanding as he is not aware that the stories are valued by Christians regardless of their literal truth.

Extract from Ibrar's improved answer

The writers of the Bible explain the idea of God as creator in the first two chapters of Genesis as well as in other areas of the Bible. Many theologians believe that there are in fact two creation stories in Genesis. Genesis 1 presents a transcendent picture of the creator God. He is able to create by word alone, this shows the omnipotence of God. He does not need to do anything other than to speak and things happen. Some scholars date this creation story to the Babylonian exile. The Jews were banished from their homeland. Yet, in the midst of this, the writer of Genesis 1 is able to demonstrate the superiority of Yahweh, their God. Genesis 1 also shows the benevolence of God, he is a creator who delights in creating varied types of life. He gives human beings authority to rule over the earth.

The story of Genesis 2 is slightly different. The image portrayed here is of an immanent God, a God who walks in the garden with Adam and Eve and desires to be close to his creation. Here God creates out of existing material and works like a master craftsman to mould Adam and then Eve. The creator sets boundaries and makes it clear what he expects of his creation. Adam and Eve are told that they can eat whatever they like except the fruit of the Tree of Knowledge and, although they disobey God, this does not end their relationship with their creator.

Modern thinkers have different views as to how the Bible writers present God as creator. Some thinkers believe that these stories are literally true, whereas others believe that they are poetic and symbolically present spiritual truth.

Examiner says

This is a much improved answer; there is no need to retell the stories of Creation. Ibrar has picked up on the word 'writers'; he is actually answering the question and showing good knowledge of technical terms.

Examiner says

A number of key points addressed. Some of these may have been worth unpacking in a bit more detail. For example, Ibrar could have also looked at other parts of the Bible, such as references to Creation in the Psalms. Nevertheless, this has the makings of a very good answer to the question.

Traditional arguments for the existence of God

Just because the universe is amazing, does there have to be a **designer** God who is still alive today? If evolution is the answer, does that **automatically** rule out a designer God?

In this chapter you will learn:

■ how to explain both Anselm's and Descartes' version of the Ontological Argument and assess the challenges from Gaunilo and Kant

■ how to explain the Teleological Argument from Aquinas and Paley and assess the challenges from Hume, Mill and Darwin

■ how to explain Kant's Moral Argument and assess the challenge from Freud

■ how to explain the Cosmological Argument of Aquinas and Copleston and assess the challenges from Hume and Russell.

Just because the universe is amazing, does there have to be a **designer** God who is still alive today? If evolution is the answer, does that **automatically** rule out a designer God?

Traditional arguments for the existence of God

3.1 Anselm and the Ontological Argument

In this topic you will consider the Ontological Argument, constructed by the medieval theologian Anselm to prove the existence of God.

Anselm

St Anselm (1033–1109), who became Archbishop of Canterbury in 1093, never doubted the existence of God. This means that when he constructed his argument to prove the existence of God, he started with a concept he accepted totally. What this argument does is use reason to justify a belief. This is an *a priori* argument because it relies on knowledge gained from reasoning and not from senses.

Responding to the opening of Psalms 14 and 53 which begin 'The Fool says to himself, "There is no God,"' Anselm set out to prove the foolish atheist was wrong.

Anselm began with his definition of God, which says it is impossible for there to be a more perfect being.

> God is 'a being than which nothing greater can be conceived'.
>
> Anselm

Anselm's first argument: Proof of God's existence

Step 3

If there is no being greater than God, God must exist in reality as well as in thought.

Apply Step 2 to Step 1 and logically God must exist. The reason is that if God only existed in thought we would be able (as a result of the definition we started with) to think of something greater, that is, a real God. So if we can conceive of God it would be contradictory to say he doesn't exist.

Step 2

Something that really exists is bound to be greater than something that just exists in thought.

Think how delighted you would be if you won four million pounds on the Lottery. But wouldn't it be better if it really happened! The real thing is always greater than the version in thought.

Step 1

God is a being than which nothing greater can be conceived.

Anselm said atheists can define God even if they don't believe in him.

The Ontological Argument

This sort of argument is called **Ontological** because it is concerned with 'existence'. Anselm uses reason, not experience, to reach his conclusion that God must exist by definition. What you may have noticed is that the definition of God Anselm started with is not one that actually helps us with the meaning of the word God.

Gaunilo's criticism

The monk Gaunilo was a contemporary of Anselm, and as a member of a religious brotherhood never doubted the existence of God either but he thought Anselm's argument was flawed. Gaunilo responded with his own written argument which he called 'On Behalf of the Fool', following on from the idea of the atheist fool mentioned in the Psalms.

Firstly

> *Of God, or a being greater than all others, I could not conceive at all, except merely according to the word. An object can hardly or never be conceived according to the word alone…*

As Gaunilo points out, we are human and all our experience gained through the senses has shown us that things are not perfect. They always have the potential to improve. It is impossible for humans to think of a fully perfect being.

Secondly

Gaunilo also said, if a friend told him about the most perfect lost island that was better than anywhere else in the world, he could imagine that. If his friend then went on to say, the island would be even better if it was real rather than just in Gaunilo's imagination, then, according to Anselm's argument, that island must exist. But, Gaunilo said, just because you can conceive of something, it doesn't make it exist. Facts are needed. Gaunilo made his point by arguing that if Anselm's argument can be used to prove the existence of a non-existent island, it's flawed! You can't move from thought to reality.

MAKING LINKS A01 skills

Can you detect the influence of Plato on Anselm? In earlier writings Anselm described God as perfect goodness which causes goodness in everything he creates. Draw a Venn diagram to compare Plato's Forms with Anselm's argument for the existence of God.

ACTIVITY A01 skills

Write a paragraph describing your perfect holiday island. If you apply Anselm's argument to this, where would it lead you?

ACTIVITY A02 skills

Write an email to Anselm from Gaunilo setting out his criticism of Anselm's argument for the existence of God.

Or role play an interview between Anselm and Gaunilo in which Gaunilo attempts to destroy the logical argument Anselm has constructed. Anselm fights back!

3.2 Anselm and his supporters fight back

In this topic you will look at Anselm's defence of his first Ontological Argument and the second part he developed.

Anselm responds to Gaunilo

Anselm countered Gaunilo's criticism (on page 43), by saying you couldn't possibly compare God with an island because you are not comparing like with like. We know that an island had a beginning and it is likely to come to an end one day. The word for this unstable state of existence is **contingent**, which means that something can exist, or need not exist. An island could come into existence as a result of many factors like the geological structure, weather conditions or perhaps human activity. An island certainly doesn't have an eternal existence, we can visualise it like Anselm said: 'having a beginning and an end and composed of parts.' By contrast, he argued, God is unique and eternal. He is a necessary being.

When the term '**necessary**' is used in a philosophical argument, it means that it is logically impossible for the opposite case to be true. A necessary truth might be 'a widow is a woman whose husband has died'. That has to be true. If you change any part of the sentence it would be nonsense. For example if 'woman' was changed to 'man' that would be inaccurate. If 'died' was altered to 'separated' or 'married' or anything else, it would be wrong. By definition this sentence has to be true.

Anselm's second argument – Necessary existence

Continuing with the a priori argument developed from his previous definition of God as 'a being than which nothing greater can be conceived,' Anselm asked:

Which is the greater?

> A God who can be thought of as not existing

or

> A God who cannot be thought of as not existing

The answer has to be the second. So that, Anselm argued in his book *Proslogion* written before his exchange with Gaunilo, proves logically that God's existence is necessary.

> *Therefore, if that than which nothing greater can be conceived exists in the understanding alone, the very being than which nothing greater can be conceived is one than which a greater can be conceived. But obviously this is impossible. Hence there is no doubt that there exists a being than which nothing greater can be conceived, and it exists both in the understanding and in the reality.*
>
> Anselm (*Proslogion*)

ACTIVITY **A01** skills

Sum up Gaunilo's attack on Anselm in about 100 words.

KEY WORD

Contingent means that something might or might not happen.

KEY WORD

Necessary refers to something which logically must be true.

ACTIVITY **A01** skills

Review Anselm's definition of God and explain why God is a necessary being. Then write Anselm's quotation from *Proslogion* in your own words.

God is a necessary being

Anselm has constructed an argument where it is necessary for God to exist according to his definition. This type of sentence is called **analytic**. (The subject of the sentence) GOD = the greatest possible being (this second half of the sentence is called the predicate). Both halves of this sentence are linked. The definition of the subject necessarily includes the predicate just as in the earlier sentence about the widow. What is 'the greatest possible being'? Well there is only one answer. The same is true in this context if you ask 'What is God?' The answer has to be 'the greatest possible being'.

◼ If you think about a mountain does it necessarily have a valley?

Anselm's supporters

The seventeenth-century French philosopher Descartes (1596–1650) may not have actually read Anselm's argument for the existence of God, but he developed his own along similar lines. Descartes started with his definition that 'God is a supremely perfect being'. He argued that a being which is the most perfect possible would necessarily contain all the attributes of perfection. These he said included things such as beauty, goodness, existence and being eternal. Therefore God must exist.

Existence is a necessary part of the meaning of God, Descartes stated.

> *God is the most perfect being possible, so he has all perfections.*
> *Existence is a perfection.*
> *As the most perfect being, God must exist.*

To illustrate his argument, Descartes used analytic sentences. He said that if you talk about a triangle it has to mean a shape with three sides and three angles. In the same way, if you think of a mountain, there has to be a valley. Just as a mountain and a valley are inseparable so, he reasoned, is the notion of God and existence.

Modern supporters of the Ontological Argument

Because the chief exponents of the Ontological Argument lived hundreds of years ago, you might be forgiven for thinking this style of argument is out of date. However, in the late twentieth century, philosophers such as Norman Malcolm and Charles Hartshorne constructed Ontological Arguments. More recently Alvin Plantinga, John Hick and John Polkinghorne have formulated Ontological Arguments.

ACTIVITY A01 skills

Outline Anselm's total argument for the existence of God.

How convincing do you find it?

KEY WORD

Analytic: a statement that is true by definition. No evidence is needed.

KEY WORD

Synthetic: a statement in which the predicate is not a necessary part of the description of the subject, e.g. 'The mermaid has a large comb.'

ACTIVITY A01 skills

Compose three analytic sentences of your own that have to be true. Then compose three sentences that are **synthetic** to prove the case.

FURTHER RESEARCH

Research one Ontological Argument a twentieth-century philosopher has produced and present it to the group. Choose from one of those mentioned on the left.

A01 skills

3.3 Critics of the Ontological Argument

In this topic you will examine some of the challenges that have been levelled at the Ontological Argument, particularly those from the philosopher Kant.

The German philosopher Kant (1724–1804) was the first person to name this type of argument for the existence of God, which relies on the meaning of words and logic, as ontological. He did not doubt the existence of God but he believed the Ontological Argument was deeply flawed. As you will see on pages 60–62 he offered his own Moral Argument.

Kant's first criticism: God has necessary existence

Kant agreed with Descartes' reasoning that by definition a three-sided figure must be a triangle, but pointed out that if you don't have a triangle in the first place, then it won't have three sides anyway.

> *To posit a triangle, and yet to reject its three angles, is self-contradictory; but there is no contradiction in rejecting the triangle together with its three angles.*
>
> Kant

You can see we are back to the analytic sentence. (Remind yourself of the relationship between subject and predicate in an analytic sentence. See page 45)

Applying this reasoning to the existence of God, Kant argued that if you believe in God, it is logical to think his existence is necessary. However, the fact that you can define something in an analytic way doesn't necessarily make it real. A popular example of this is 'A unicorn has one horn'. That may be true but it does not make unicorns exist.

Kant's second criticism: Existence is not a predicate

Kant accepted that there are some sentences where the subject cannot be thought of without the predicate – in other words they contain information that is inseparable from the subject, for example, a house has a door. Two plus two equals four. But God and existence, he said, was not like that because it was quite possible to think of a being who doesn't exist.

He also pointed out that existing in reality may not add anything to an idea that exists in the imagination. Kant gave the example of coins that is shown in the picture. Kant pointed out that you do not do anything to the *description* of an object by saying it is real not imaginary. An imaginary pile of a hundred gold coins will have the same number in it as a real pile. All you are doing by saying this object really exists is asserting there is a real example of it, you are not improving the *description* of it.

▮ Kant asked whether there was more money in an imaginary pile of a hundred coins or a real pile of a hundred coins.

Because the existence, or non-existence, of real money adds nothing to the number of coins, he said existence is not a predicate. So if we can't accept existence as a predicate when talking of coins, why should we make a special case when talking about something like God?

Kant's line of argument has been denied. Some supporters of the Ontological Argument point out that there is a big difference in what you can buy with real coins and imaginary ones, so existence is a predicate.

A weak definition

Some critics of the Ontological Argument have pointed out that the definition Anselm began with was flawed. You may have noticed when you compared your definition of God with Anselm's on page 42 that the approaches were different. It is likely that you were trying to give meaning to the word, whereas what Anselm actually gave was a quality. This was Gaunilo's point, when he said that whilst he could give God a name, he couldn't attempt to define God in words. How can you define something that you have not experienced through the senses? Since God is a spiritual being, not only is that difficult to experience in our earthly world, there is also the problem that human language is limited. We do not have the words to describe spiritual experiences.

Let's evaluate the Ontological Argument

As a method of argument, the Ontological Argument relies entirely on analytic reasoning. The definition of words and the use of language are what drive this argument forward. There is nothing empirical in it, which is why some people find the Ontological Argument weak.

Traditional arguments for the existence of God

3.4 Aquinas' Cosmological Argument

In this topic you will examine Aquinas' argument to prove the existence of God and Hume's criticism of it.

Aquinas said:

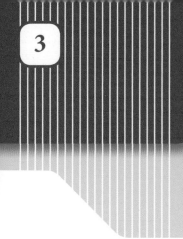

Nothing comes from nothing

The universe exists, so something must have made it

That can only be God

▌ The Cosmological Argument looks at the universe around us and seeks an explanation for its existence.

ACTIVITY A01 skills

Give a brief summary of the conclusions reached by Aristotle about the universe.

The Dominican friar Thomas Aquinas (1224–74) developed an argument the ancient Greeks used for the existence of God. He began in the natural world of the senses and reasoned from it, making this is an a posteriori argument.

FOR DEBATE A02 skills

Nothing comes from nothing. That's impossible.

Hume's Criticisms of Aquinas

The eighteenth-century philosopher David Hume (1711–1776) was an empiricist. He required facts, in other words knowledge derived from our five senses. Hume considered Aquinas' argument, starting with the existence of the universe. Whilst accepting the universe exists, Hume asked if it had to have a beginning. Just because everything in our world is governed by cause and effect, that doesn't mean the universe had to have a cause. Could it not be infinite?

> If the material world rests upon a similar ideal world, this ideal world must rest upon some other; and so on, without end
>
> Hume

Hume also questioned the existence of God. God is 'an arbitrary act of the mind,' he claimed. By this Hume meant that although Aquinas' argument was perfectly logical, it did not mean it was necessarily true. Pushing his case further, Hume suggested maybe there wasn't one Prime Mover. Could there not be several acting together like a committee?

Hume challenged the idea of cause and effect, saying that it might be the case that what we perceive as causation is simply statistical conjunction. For example, a person goes up to somebody and pushes them over. What we see is a person walking up to another person and pushing them. We also see the

AQUINAS' ARGUMENT

Fifth Way

Fourth Way

First way: Motion

Evidence: Everything in existence is in motion or has the potential to change, for example, humans develop, grow old and die. Wood has the potential to be made into something or to be burnt. Aquinas said all change is caused by something. Because nothing can move of its own accord, there has to be a Prime Mover. (Look at the dominoes on page 22) That must be God.

Second Way: Causation

Evidence: Cause and effect are natural in our world. Whatever happens is caused by something else. It would be illogical to say something can cause itself because that means it was there before it began. There needs to be a first cause. That is God.

Third Way: A necessary being

Evidence: Nothing in our world is permanent. Everything is contingent; it exists but could equally well not exist. That means it is possible there was a time when nothing existed. Since we know it is not possible for nothing to come from nothing, that means there had to be something in existence. There must be a necessary being, which all the contingent beings came from. That is God.

second person fall over. Because we have seen such things before, we interpret the action to mean the effect of pushing a person is to cause another to fall over.

Hume asked why the Prime Mover has to be identified with the Christian God. If we base our argument on our human experience of cause and effect, would it not be more logical to suggest a world created by male and female gods who are born and who will die?

J. L. Mackie said that Aquinas regarded the causes of the universe as a series of hooks hanging one below the other from a fixed point on the wall. If the wall was taken away the chain would fall apart, but he argued it might be a case of infinite regress. It is possible for a chain of hooks to be infinite, with no first hook attached to the wall and thus no Prime Mover.

Traditional arguments for the existence of God

3.5 Does the universe need explaining?

In this topic you will study a significant twentieth-century debate on the Cosmological Argument.

Copleston vs Russell

In 1948, two philosophers were invited to take part in a radio debate about the existence of God. One was a Catholic priest and Professor of the History of Philosophy, Father Frederick Copleston (1907–1994), the other a member of the English aristocracy, Lord Bertrand Russell (1872–1970) who became one of the greatest British philosophers and described himself as agnostic. Their discussion centred on the Cosmological Argument for the cause of the universe.

They started by agreeing on a definition of God as 'a supreme personal being – distinct from the world and creator of the world.'

Below are some of the key parts from their debate.

Oh yes it does!

This was Copleston's view on whether the existence of the universe could be explained.

Copleston argued:

> *… we know there are at least some beings in the world which do not contain in themselves the reason for their existence. For example, I depend on my parents, and now on the air, and on food, and so on.*
>
> *… the world is simply the real or imagined totality or aggregate of individual objects, none of which contain in themselves alone the reason for their existence. There isn't any world distinct from the objects which form it, any more than the human race is something apart from the members. Therefore, I should say, since objects or events exist, and since no object of experience contains within itself reason of its existence, this reason, the totality of objects, must have a reason external to itself. That reason must be an existent being. Well, this being is either itself the reason for its own existence, or it is not. If it is, well and good. If it is not, then we must proceed farther. But if we proceed to infinity in that sense, then there's no explanation of existence at all. So I should say, in order to explain existence, we must come to a being which contains within itself the reason for its own existence.*
>
> *Only a contingent being can have a cause. God is His own sufficient reason; and He is not cause of Himself.*

ACTIVITY   A01 skills

Bullet-point Copleston's argument then compare his points with those of Aquinas to see where there are similarities.

STRETCH & CHALLENGE   A01 skills

Find out what Leibniz meant by 'sufficient reason'. Then explain to the group how he used it to support the Cosmological Argument.

Oh no it doesn't!

That was Russell's answer to the question that opened this topic. He summed up his argument:

> I should say that the universe is just there, and that's all.

He went on to say:

> … I don't admit the idea of a necessary being and I don't admit that there is any particular meaning in calling other beings "contingent". These phrases don't for me have a significance except within a logic that I reject.
>
> … you ask whether I consider that the universe is unintelligible. I shouldn't say unintelligible – I think it is without explanation.
>
> 'Does the cause of the world exist?' is a question that has meaning. But if you say 'Yes, God is the cause of the world' you're using God as a proper name; then 'God exists' will not be a statement that has meaning … for suppose you take as your subject 'the existent round-square', it would look like an analytic proposition that 'the existent round-square exists', but it doesn't exist.
>
> The whole concept of cause is one we derive from our observation of particular things; I see no reason whatsoever to suppose that … the world as a whole must have a cause. For that assumption I see no ground whatever.
>
> I can illustrate what seems to me your fallacy. Every man who exists has a mother, and it seems to me your argument is that therefore the human race must have a mother, but obviously the human race hasn't a mother – that's a different logical sphere.

Russell turned to twentieth-century developments in theoretical physics to support his case:

> As for things not having a cause, the physicists assure us that individual quantum transitions in atoms have no cause … a physicist looks for causes; that does not necessarily imply that there are causes everywhere. A man may look for gold without assuming that there is gold everywhere; if he finds gold, well and good, if he doesn't he's had bad luck. The same is true when the physicists look for causes.

Copleston replied that scientific research proved the opposite.

> I cannot see how science could be conducted on any other assumption than that of order and intelligibility in nature. The physicist presupposes … that there is some sense in investigating nature and looking for the causes of events, just as the detective presupposes that there is some sense in looking for the cause of a murder.

ACTIVITY A01+A02 Skills

Bullet-point Russell's arguments. How effective do you think they are in demolishing Copleston's case?

STRETCH & CHALLENGE

Read a full transcript of this radio debate and decide who offered the most convincing argument. A01+A02 Skills

You could role-play this debate as 'Philosophy: Match of the Day' with a commentator analysing the argument.

ACTIVITY A01 skills

Draw a diagram to display Copleston's Cosmological Argument or show the sequence of the argument as a strip cartoon.

3.6 The Design Argument

In this topic you will look at Aquinas and Paley's argument that the design of the world proves there is a God.

Teleological Argument

The Teleological Argument, also known as the Design Argument, is concerned with the reason why the world functions in an orderly and intelligent manner. This a posteriori argument begins with the natural world and, by use of analogy, goes on to prove the existence of God. Some philosophers point out that the argument actually has two parts.

There is the argument *to design*

There is the argument *from design*

Aquinas

We encountered three of Aquinas' Five Ways on page 49. This fifth one states there is evidence for the existence of God in the world around us.

> *We see that things which lack knowledge, such as natural bodies, act for an end, and this is evident from their acting always, or nearly always, in the same way, so as to obtain the best results. Hence it is plain that they achieve their end not fortuitously, but designedly. Now whatever lacks knowledge cannot move towards an end, unless it be directed by some being endowed with knowledge and intelligence… Therefore some intelligent being exists by whom all natural things are directed to their end; and this being we call God.*

Aquinas said that many objects in the world without innate intelligence perform in a way that achieves the best possible results. The reason for this is because they have been designed that way. He used the analogy of an arrow. The reason the arrow reaches its target is that an archer directs it there. By taking that example across into the natural world, Aquinas says the reason objects in our world perform their job efficiently is that they were designed that way. That proves there is an intelligent designer behind everything in our world. That designer is God.

If you analyse the construction of this argument, you can see that Aquinas began with an empirical fact, namely that everything in the world is nearly always adapted to fulfil its function. He then moved on by way of an analogy, to prove his point. What happens if you don't think you can compare an arrow with something like the life cycle of a butterfly? Where does that leave the argument?

■ This is an extremely expensive designer watch. What do we mean by 'designer watch' and why do people rate such things so highly?

Paley's watch

William Paley (1743–1805), an eighteenth-century theologian, put forward this famous example of the Teleological Argument.

> *In crossing a heath, suppose I pitched my foot against a stone, and were asked how the stone came to be there, I might possibly answer, that for anything I knew to the contrary it had lain there for ever.*

However, he says if he found a watch on the ground, this sort of explanation wouldn't do because a watch is clearly an intricate piece of workmanship. Its parts are designed *'and put together for a purpose, e.g. that they are so formed and adjusted as to produce motion, and that motion so regulated as to point out the hour of the day.'* If any of the parts had been shaped differently or put together in another order the watch would not work. All the parts of the watch, he concluded, has been designed and assembled in the right order by a watchmaker for the purpose of keeping time.

Now here comes the analogy: 'Every indication of contrivance, every manifestation of design, which existed in the watch, exists in the works of nature.'

Taking his argument one stage further, Paley moved to the natural world and stated the same efficient design is found there. He chose the human eye as an example of a complex mechanism designed specifically for the purpose of sight yet lacking its own intelligence.

ACTIVITY

A01 skills

Write Paley's analogy in plain English and explain how he uses this argument to prove the existence of God.

ACTIVITY

A01 skills

Apart from the human body, name four other different phenomena in the natural world that appear to be designed to function efficiently. What would Paley say that proved? What other explanations are possible?

STRETCH & CHALLENGE

A02 skills

How can Aquinas be said to be arguing to design and Paley arguing from design?

3.7 Hume attacks the arguments of Aquinas and Paley

In this topic you will study the criticisms that Hume levelled at the Teleological Argument.

Although Hume wrote a few years before Paley, Hume believed that the Teleological Argument was deeply flawed and spent some time forming a response to it. Because such an 'ungodly' argument was dangerous in the eighteenth century, he used Socrates' technique of writing a dispute between several people, one of whom makes the point for Hume. He also took care to ensure his work would not be published until after his death.

It is a weak analogy

Hume's whole argument hinges on the fact that comparing God, the creator of the world, to anything on earth is not a valid analogy. Let's look in detail at his argument:

> There are other parts of the universe (besides machines of human invention) which bear still a greater resemblance to the fabric of the world . . . these parts are animals and vegetables.

It is clear that Hume would not have accepted the comparison with Paley's watch. He preferred consideration of organic objects that can grow and develop on their own:

> You must acknowledge that it is impossible for us to tell, from our limited views, whether this system contains any great faults or deserves any praise if compared to other possible – or even real – systems.

Because we live inside the world and don't know any other worlds to compare it with, Hume thought humans were not in a position to make a valid judgement. We cannot step outside the universe and see what makes it tick.

> From observing the growth of a hair can we learn anything concerning the generation of a man? Would the manner of a leaf's blowing, even though perfectly known, afford us any instruction concerning the vegetation of a tree?
>
> The world, for aught he knows, is very faulty and imperfect, compared to a superior standard, and was only the first rude essay of some infant Deity who afterwards abandoned it, ashamed of his lame performance; it is the work only of some dependent, inferior Deity and is the object of derision to his superiors …

This daring argument suggests that our world with its faults may actually be a prototype. Hume argued that once you say the attributes of God are infinite, then all sorts of things are possible. Because we live on the earth and don't know anything else, how do we know this is an example of a perfect world?

Our universe might not be the perfect product of a divine craftsman. Extending the machine image, Hume pointed out that machines that go wrong are abandoned, or altered until they function properly:

> *Many worlds might have been botched and bungled, throughout eternity, ere this system was struck out; much labour lost; many fruitless trials made and a slow but continued improvement carried on during infinite ages in the art of world-making.*

What has happened to God, the supreme being, now?

Arguing from the natural world, Hume said we see disasters and suffering which might mean the designer of the universe was not a loving personal God. Instead he might be one who *'has no more regard to good above ill than to heat above cold or drought above moisture'.*

We know that machines are made by humans because we have seen it happen, but no-one has seen a world being made by any being.

Likening building the world to building a house, Hume suggested there might actually be a team of builders involved, each having different skills. Who is to say there was not a team of gods involved in the construction of the universe?

■ What is the difference between a cabbage and a machine? No, it's not the opening line of a joke! According to Paley it would be reasonable to use these objects interchangeably in the argument. What will Hume say and why?

FURTHER RESEARCH

Hume suggested the Epicurean Thesis as a possible explanation for the design of the universe. Epicurus puts forward the idea of infinite time, in which there is a huge but finite number of particles moving about, going through every possible combination. If any one combination happens to represent a stable order, it must occur – this would have the appearance of design. Thus, apparent design could happen at random, without the need to infer a designer. Find out more about this argument.

ACTIVITY  A01+A02 Skills

Summarise Hume's criticisms then rank them. Write a response to his criticism from a theist.

3.1

MAKING LINKS

Hume said the reason plants and animals appear to be well-adjusted to their environment is that those that didn't function properly died out. Can you see the link with Darwin's Natural Selection here? See page 56–57.

3.8 The Big Challenge

In this topic we will look at the great challenge to the Teleological Argument that came in the nineteenth century from Charles Darwin and his contemporary John Stuart Mill.

❚ How does a scene like this challenge the idea of God as the designer of the universe?

ACTIVITY A01+A02 Skills

In the passage on page 57, Darwin refers to the weakness of arguing from an analogy. What is the analogy he uses? Explain why Darwin says Paley's argument from design does not work.

ACTIVITY A01 skills

Bullet-point Darwin's case against the Teleological Argument.

STRETCH & CHALLENGE A02 skills

Darwin's case against the Design Argument is argued by analogy on page 57. How valid do you think his analogy is?

Charles Darwin (1809–1882)

Darwin knew Hume's writings and admitted to reading them around the time he developed his Theory of Evolution. Darwin published this theory in 1859 in a book entitled 'On the Origin of Species' and in many ways, Darwin was offering scientific evidence that supported Hume's arguments of eighty years earlier. Using a posteriori argument, Darwin looked at the world around him and reasoned why things were as they were. His conclusions challenged many existing beliefs about God and humanity. Darwin himself was an agnostic.

Theory of Natural Selection

From scientific observation, Darwin noted that plants and animals changed as they adapted to their environment. Those that failed to adapt did not survive. Those that survived went on to breed so their characteristics were passed on to the next generation. You may remember that Hume had said one reason why objects in our natural world appeared to be so well-designed is because those that aren't fail to survive. (See page 55).

Darwin produced evidence to show this was the case and that change had come about gradually and by chance. Although the world we see around us has the appearance of design, the intricacies of nature can actually be explained by evolution. It is simply the survival of the fittest organism. This needs no external being or designer.

Darwin was only too aware that he had challenged the Teleological Argument as this extract from his writings shows:

> The old argument from design in nature, as given by Paley, which formerly seemed to me so conclusive, fails, now that the law of natural selection has been discovered. We can no longer argue that, for instance, the beautiful hinge of a bivalve shell must have been made by an intelligent being, like the hinge of a door by a man. There seems to be no more design in the variability of organic beings and in the action of natural selection, than in the course which the wind blows.

Darwin was also aware of the theological implication of his ideas as this passage from one of his letters shows:

> An innocent and good man stands under a tree and is killed by a flash of lightning. Do you believe that God designedly killed this man? Many and most persons do believe this; I can't and don't. If you believe so, do you believe that when a swallow snaps up a gnat that God designed that that particular swallow snaps up that particular gnat at that particular instant? I believe that the man and the gnat are in the same predicament. If the death of neither man nor gnat are designed, I see no reason to believe that their first birth or production should be necessarily designed.

Darwin's theory of evolution by natural selection suggests that humans are rising in the animal kingdom as they develop the power of rational thought. This contrasts with the account in Genesis of humans beginning perfect and falling into sin.

John Stuart Mill joined the debate

Mill (1806–1873) knew Darwin's work well. Looking at the natural world containing scenes such as those in the photograph, Mill wrote:

> In sober truth, nearly all the things which men are hanged or imprisoned for doing to one another, are nature's every day performances. Killing, the most criminal act recognized by human laws, Nature does once to every being that lives; and in a large proportion of cases, after protracted tortures such as only the greatest monsters whom we read of ever purposely inflicted on their living fellow-creatures.

If progress comes through pain and suffering, what does that say about the nature of the designer of the universe, he asked.

> For however offensive the proposition may appear to many religious persons, they should be willing to look in the face the undeniable fact, that the order of nature … if made wholly by such a Being … could only be as a designedly imperfect work, which man, in his limited sphere, is to exercise justice and benevolence in amending.

FOR DEBATE A02 skills

The Theory of Natural Selection doesn't weaken the Teleological Argument. It strengthens it because it shows God the Designer in action.

ACTIVITY A01 skills

Compare Mill's view of God with the attributes that appeared on pages 32–33.

MAKING LINKS

Mill's observations here will have a place in the problem of evil on pages 70–71.

STRETCH & CHALLENGE A02 A01 skills

Research how a modern philosopher such as Richard Swinburne supports the Teleological Argument and the atheist zoologist Richard Dawkins criticises it. Give a presentation to the group.

or

Find out about an argument called the Anthropic Principle developed by F.R. Tennant in the 1930s. Present your findings to the group.

3.9 Comparing arguments

In this topic you will revise your knowledge of the arguments about the existence of God.

ACTIVITY **A01** skills

Choose one of the arguments displayed here and produce a presentation that would help members of the group refresh their knowledge of the argument. You might like to end the presentation with a quick quiz to see who was listening!

Aquinas' Ontological Argument

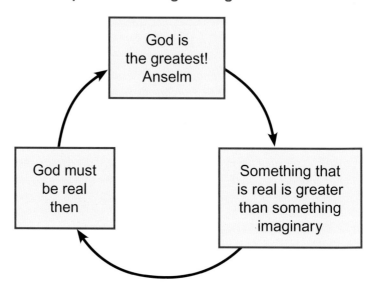

Aquinas' Cosmological Argument

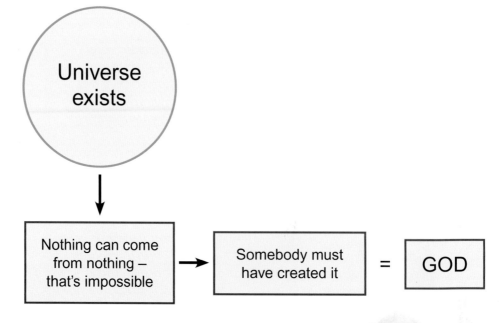

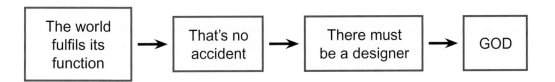

Aquinas' Teleological Argument

| The world fulfils its function | → | That's no accident | → | There must be a designer | → | GOD |

3.10 Kant's Moral Argument

In this topic you will consider Kant's argument that because we all possess a sense of morality that suggests there is a God.

▌ Think of three different reasons why this girl goes to see her granny regularly.

Kant's Moral Argument for the existence of God is an unusual argument because it doesn't prove God exists, it only points to the probability that God exists. Kant did not think it was possible for human intellect to prove the existence of something totally beyond anything we have experienced. Instead he turned to 'the moral law within us' for evidence.

Visiting Granny

Consider the situation in the picture. Sophie visits her grandmother in the old people's home every Thursday after college. Her friends wonder why she bothers. Granny hasn't got any money to leave her and the reception Sophie gets is very unpredictable. Occasionally granny is pleased to see her, but more often Sophie is greeted by complaints that she doesn't visit often enough and is too busy enjoying herself to think about her poor old gran. There have even been times when granny has slept right through Sophie's visit and never noticed her. So why does Sophie visit when she gains no pleasure from it? The answer is that she feels it is her duty towards another human being.

> *Good will shines forth like a precious jewel.*
>
> Kant

Kant's moral argument

Kant said there is universal agreement that some actions are right and others wrong. It doesn't matter what culture, circumstances or period of history we are talking about. Actions like murder and rape, for example, are always bad. This, Kant said, shows the existence of an objective moral law that everybody is aware of.

Not only are we aware of this moral law, Kant said we feel an obligation to obey it because it is the rational thing to do. To discover the right action we must apply moral reason, this will reveal the moral law and gives us the **categorical imperative** which we should obey (see page 107).

Duty, Kant said, is doing a good action for no other reason than we know it is our duty. Sophie visits her granny simply because it is her duty as a granddaughter. Duty is not a response to threats or rewards. If Sophie acted because her mother nagged her or because it made her feel good or she did it out of love, Kant said this would not be a virtuous action. Virtue can only be duty for duty's sake.

Why are we moral?

According to Kant, humans are obliged to carry out virtuous actions from a sense of duty, not because they expect a reward. Indeed we know from experience that whilst we can carry out a virtuous action, there is no guarantee it will always lead to happiness. Yet it is logical for a virtuous action to be rewarded by happiness eventually. This state, when virtue and happiness do come together, Kant called the **Summum Bonum**. Kant reasoned that because the summum bonum is rarely achieved in one lifetime, then logically there must be an afterlife in which to achieve it.

Kant considered his argument had three necessary parts, which he called **three postulates**.

Three Postulates of Morality

Freedom	Immortality	God
Kant said a course of action is only moral if a person is free to carry it out. Sophie exercised her free will, when deciding to visit her grandmother, without rewards, threats or pressures. Also she was able to undertake the visit. If she had been unable to visit through lack of transport or illness then no duty would exist.	Experience tells us that virtuous actions are not always rewarded by happiness, indeed they may attract criticism or pain. Since perfect virtue ought to result in perfect happiness, then it must exist. Because it doesn't happen in this life, it follows that God must provide it in the next life.	For Kant it follows logically that if there is another life in which humans can achieve immortality, then this means God is the necessary connection between virtue and happiness which is implied by the summum bonum.

Kant's Moral Argument for the existence of God

It is logical for perfect virtue to be rewarded by perfect happiness.	→	Humans cannot achieve the summum bonum without God and an afterlife.	→	God must exist to provide the summum bonum.

KEY WORDS

Categorical imperative involves making a moral decision from a sense of duty without any consideration of the outcome.

Summum bonum is the state of supreme good when virtue and happiness come together.

Postulate is something which is an assumption; it is probable but not provable.

ACTIVITY
A01 skills

Explain why it would be wrong to describe Kant's Moral Argument as proof of the existence of God.

STRETCH & CHALLENGE
A02 skills

Explain what Kant meant when he wrote:

'It is impossible to conceive of anything at all in the world, or even out of it, which can be taken as good without qualification, except a good will.'

Do you agree with him?

3.11 Weighing up the Moral Argument

In this topic you will investigate Freud's challenge to the Moral Argument and evaluate the different viewpoints.

Freud

Sigmund Freud (1856–1939) had a huge impact on twentieth-century thought when he introduced the idea that our behaviour is influenced by psychological causes and not by any divine intervention. As an atheist, he argued that any mystical experiences people might have were actually regressions to the comforts of their childhood rather than an awareness of any external force.

He accepted that we have a conscience but disagreed that it came from God. In Freud's view our conscience is a product of our unconscious mind, which he called our **superego**. This superego knows what we should or shouldn't do.

Freud looked at a person's start in life. As a baby develops, it gradually gains a sense of self-awareness and its own identity, which Freud termed our **ego**. Parents, teachers and other figures in authority all play their part in teaching us the sort of behaviour that is acceptable in society. They praise right behaviour and punish wrong. We continually internalise the information we have learned and reinforce it with disapproval or approval for similar actions. This becomes our personal moral code, which Freud calls our superego and others may call our conscience. Freud saw superegos as blank sheets of paper which society writes the rules on.

▌ Freud believes our conscience is like a moral policeman watching and judging our actions.

> **KEY WORD**
>
> **Ego**: the conscious self, the personality that the outside world sees.

> **KEY WORD**
>
> **Superego**: the subconscious set of moral controls given us by outside influences like the rules of society.

Freud sees the superego as existing independently of our basic wants and desires and sometimes at odds with rational thought. Our superego is like a moral policeman, continually watching, advising and judging our every move when it comes to moral decisions. We have the freedom to choose whether we act on the information the superego provides. Acting in accordance with the superego makes us feel virtuous; going against it makes us feel guilty.

It is worth noting that whilst Freud recognises what influences the superego, he does not explain where the superego comes from.

KANT: morality is something everybody reasons for themselves.

FREUD: our superego is the result of experience and upbringing.

Evaluating the Moral Argument

ACTIVITY A01+A02 Skills

Copy the points below onto slips of paper, then sort them into those which support the Moral Argument and those which criticise it. You may wish to add points of your own to either pile.

- The Moral Argument is one of probability, not certainty.
- There is no logical reason why our sense of right and wrong comes from God.
- Moral behaviour doesn't have to be rewarded by happiness.
- You can't prove morality comes from the superego.
- If having a sense of morality is a normal part of life then there is no need for a God.
- Perhaps God uses the superego to give us morality.
- Different societies have different ideas about what is right and what is wrong.
- Examining the motives for an action is not enough, the results matter too.
- Just because different cultures have slightly different rules doesn't mean there isn't a Moral Law.
- There is no logical link between God and the afterlife. There could be a natural migration of souls as in Hindu reincarnation.

FURTHER RESEARCH A01 skills

Research the modern philosopher Richard Swinburne's arguments about Moral Law and present a brief account of his argument to the class.

ACTIVITY A01 skills

Write the FAQ section about the Moral Argument to go on a philosophy website.

ACTIVITY A01 skills

Produce a revision leaflet on the Moral Argument that would help you prepare for an exam.

ExamCafé
Relax, refresh, result!

Relax and prepare

The Cosmological, Teleological and Moral Arguments

Katherine

I never truly understood this topic. I should have done more work on it or picked another question in the exam.

Rachel

I'm well pleased with my mark. The topic did my head in at first but I read the sections in the student book and on a revision website. Then the things that the teacher had said started to make sense.

Mustafa

I had to make sure I knew which argument was which. I did this by pinning spider diagrams to my bedroom wall which showed each of the key thinkers on the arguments.

Examiner's tips: the Seven Deadly Sins

Here are seven things to avoid on these topics:

1. Don't confuse the Cosmological and Teleological Arguments: the Cosmological Argument asks about the origin of the 'cosmos', in plain terms: 'how come the world exists at all?' The Teleological Argument looks at design and asks, 'how come the world is so ordered and intelligent?'

2. Don't oversimplify Aquinas: Aquinas actually has three Cosmological Arguments based on movement/change, causation and contingency. Are you clear on each of these?

3. Don't forget Mill: Mill's observations about evil and its implications for the designer are often overlooked.

4. Don't make it a biology exam: answers about Darwin need to focus on the implications for the Teleological Argument, not just explain evolution.

5. It's not a psychology exam either: don't just describe Freud's psychology if you are asked about his views on the Moral Argument.

6. It's not even an ethics exam! Don't spend too much on ethics: Kant's moral argument does link in to his ethics but don't focus too much on this.

7. The Moral Argument is not a proof: at least as far as Kant is concerned. It is a probable argument so don't start your essay by saying that Kant proved God's existence

Revision checklist for the Ontological Argument

In order to do well on this topic you will need to:

▷ Be able to explain both Anselm and Descartes' version of the Ontological Argument.
▷ Understand Gaunilo's challenge to the argument (perfect island).
▷ Understand Kant's criticism of the argument; existence is not a predicate.
▷ Explain why both Anselm and Descartes think that God *has to* exist.
▷ Assess each of the four thinkers studied.

Key points to remember

The Ontological Argument is different from the other arguments in two ways:

▷ Firstly, it is based completely on logic, not experience. It is like a mathematical or logical puzzle.
▷ Secondly, this means there is only one possible answer: God has to exist. The other arguments rarely claim to give this level of proof.

Revision checklist for the Cosmological, Teleological and Moral Arguments

In order to do well on these topics you will need to:

▷ Be able to explain both Aquinas and Copleston's versions of the Cosmological Argument.
▷ Understand the criticisms of the argument given by Hume and Russell.
▷ Assess each of the above thinkers.
▷ Assess whether the Cosmological Argument succeeds.
▷ Be able to explain both Aquinas and Paley's versions of the Teleological Argument.
▷ Explain the criticisms of the argument given by Hume, Mill and Darwin.
▷ Assess the strengths and weaknesses of each thinker's view.
▷ Assess whether the Teleological Argument is successful in proving the existence of God.
▷ Understand the Moral Argument as presented by Kant, including the concept 'summum bonum'.
▷ Understand the challenge to the Moral Argument from Freud.
▷ Assess the strengths and weaknesses of both thinkers.
▷ Assess whether the Moral Argument is successful.

Get the result!

Sample answers

Exam question

(a) Explain how Descartes developed Anselm's argument that God's existence is necessary. (25 marks)

Examiner says

A basic grasp of Anselm's first argument. Katherine has recognised that this is a question about the Ontological Argument. However, she does not pick up on the word 'necessary'. Anselm's conclusion is not that God happens to exist as you and I do, but that he *has* to exist.

Examiner says

This last paragraph highlights a common problem. Once a student knows what topic area the question is on, they feel that they have to write down everything they have learned about that topic. Look at what the question says. There are absolutely no marks for the information in this paragraph. Katherine may not have lost any marks but she does lose valuable time in giving information that is not required.

Katherine's answer

Anselm had an Ontological Argument for the existence of God. He argued that if you could think of God that meant you had an idea of God in your mind. Anselm believed that because God was the 'Greatest Conceivable Being', he would also exist in reality as it is greater to actually exist rather than just be an idea. So Anselm argued that God exists.

Gaunilo challenged this argument. He argued that he could think of a perfect island, therefore this island would have to exist. Anselm didn't agree with this and wrote a response to Gaunilo arguing that God exists whereas the perfect island doesn't. Descartes agreed with Anselm that God's existence is necessary. If you can think of God then God exists in reality as well. So Descartes believed the same as Anselm.

Kant challenged Descartes' argument and said that existence is not a predicate. This led to the argument being dismissed by most thinkers. Russell also rejected the argument. Modern thinkers such as Malcolm and Plantinga have given versions of the argument. So Descartes is not the only thinker to have developed Anselm's argument.

Examiner says

The answer gets weaker in this paragraph. Gaunilo is **not** trying to prove that the island exists. Anselm's second argument is not explained. Anselm argues that God possesses necessary existence unlike all other things. The sentence about Descartes shows that Katherine hasn't really grasped this topic.

Now your turn

Try rewriting Katherine's answer. How could you improve it? Here's how Rachel did. The answer starts here with Rachel's second paragraph: she has already explained Anselm's second Ontological Argument in her first paragraph.

Descartes' Ontological Argument builds on Anselm's second argument in focusing on the necessary existence of God. Descartes argues that a shape such as a triangle has to have certain properties: 3 sides, angles adding up to 180 degrees, etc. These things are necessary to a triangle. Descartes then considers what is necessary to the definition of God. God necessarily has all perfections. He is omnipotent, omnibenevolent and omniscient by definition. In order to fulfil the definition, God must also have the property of necessary existence. Descartes, like Anselm before him, argues that this will only work for God. We cannot apply this to perfect islands or unicorns. Descartes argues that God is the only being whose essence involves existence. In other words, the characteristics of God by definition have to include existence.

Examiner says

Rachel has really focused on the question in this paragraph. She has linked Descartes and Anselm and has written about how the Ontological Argument makes God's existence necessary. Although the two paragraph answer is slightly brief, there is enough to suggest a very high level of attainment.

Hot tips

One way to revise is to look at your specification and try writing your own questions. Remember that when the principal examiner writes the paper, he or she uses the specification to work out whether it is a fair question. The specification is what you should study and what the exam is testing. It's actually easy to come up with the questions. Once you've written a couple of questions on each topic, try answering them. You could do this activity with a friend and set and mark each other's work.

Does the existence of evil make it **impossible** for God to exist? Or is it that God can't stop it or **doesn't** want to? Could there be some other explanation?

In this chapter you will learn:

- ■ about the problem posed by evil and to understand the concepts of natural and moral evil

- ■ how to critically evaluate the theodicies of Augustine and Irenaeus concerning God's responsibility for the existence of evil

- ■ to consider the Creationist and Big Bang theories as explanations of the creation of the universe

- ■ to evaluate the contributions of Darwin and other scientists to the creation debate.

Does the existence of evil make it **impossible** for God to exist? Or is it that God can't stop it or **doesn't** want to? Could there be some other explanation?

Challenges to religious belief

4.1 What's the problem with evil?

In this topic you will think about what people mean by evil and why its existence raises problems for believers.

ACTIVITY A01 skills

Use a national and a local newspaper to cut out all the stories involving evil or suffering.

Write your own definition of evil on a post-it. Assemble the group's definitions on the board and discuss them. Can you arrive at a definition of evil you are agreed on?

ACTIVITY A01 skills

Go through your newspaper stories and decide what sort of evil each contains – natural or moral.

ACTIVITY A02 skills

Explain the discrepancies that arise between the group's definition of evil and the classical definition of God.

MAKING LINKS A01 skills

Darwin and Mill were aware of the problem evil caused believers. (See pages 56–57) What solution did they come up with?

How well is the world designed?

The Judaeo-Christian God and the view of God in ancient Greek philosophy, which we studied on pages 32–33, describe a supreme perfect being. If that is the case, what sort of universe might we expect his creativity to produce? Would you say things live up to expectations?

What is evil like?

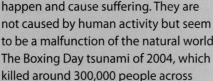

NATURAL EVIL: these are natural events, such as earthquakes and floods, which happen and cause suffering. They are not caused by human activity but seem to be a malfunction of the natural world. The Boxing Day tsunami of 2004, which killed around 300,000 people across 11 nations, is thought to be the worst natural disaster in history. On a smaller scale a tree falling on a car and injuring the occupants would be an example of natural evil.

MORAL EVIL: these are man-made activities such as murder or violence which cause suffering. A notable example would be the Holocaust in which at least six million people were murdered by the Nazis, but equally a child tormenting a dog is an example of moral evil.

It is worth remembering that some suffering may contain elements of both. The tree falling on the car may have been caused by someone leaving it in an unsafe state. Whether that was intentional, or not, is irrelevant. What matters is that it was man-made and therefore an example of moral evil.

Let's analyse the problem of evil

It is clear that religious believers do have a problem understanding how an all-powerful and all-loving God can allow evil to exist in his universe without putting a stop to it. It would also be expected that this creator God could produce a world as perfect as himself, yet natural evil suggests our world has flaws that cause humans to suffer. Equally the people God created are flawed and cause evil and suffering to each other as well as to the natural environment.

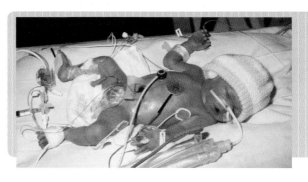

Augustine summed up the problem when he wrote: '*Either God cannot abolish evil, or He will not; if He cannot then He is not all-powerful; if He will not then He is not all-good.*'

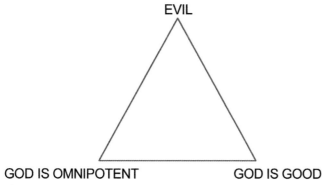

❚ The inconsistent triad

KEY WORD

The **inconsistent triad** means that a good and all-knowing God cannot exist at the same time as evil.

What logical solutions are possible?

The premise that God is a good and loving being could be wrong. The available evidence could in fact be used to argue that God is evil.

If God doesn't exist anyway that would remove the existence of good and omnipotence from the triad and solve the problem.

It is also possible that evil doesn't exist. Maybe we are misguided in interpreting events in terms of evil and suffering.

The different attributes of the Judaeo–Christian God could be wrong. Maybe God is not omnipotent and therefore not able to stop evil. Alternatively God may not be omniscient and so he is unaware of evil and suffering in the world.

Hume's solution

David Hume said only two of three points in the diagram can exist at the same time. Try out the possible combinations and explain the implications for the nature of God. He did not think the Judaeo–Christian God existed.

Hume's view is not shared by Christian philosophers. St Augustine and St Irenaeus both considered the problem of evil in a different way. Their theories are called **theodicies** because both approach the problem of evil from a position of faith and construct an argument to justify the existence of God.

KEY WORD

Theodicy literally means a justification of God. It is an attempt by philosophers to reconcile the goodness and omnipotence of God with the existence of evil. Augustine and Irenaeus are two key scholars.

4.2 The Augustinian Theodicy

In this topic you will examine the case Augustine makes for the presence of evil in the world.

Augustine in the hot seat!

Despite Augustine living between 354–430 CE we secured an interview with him. When we booked the interview he said that we should remember that he is a Christian bishop. Knowing this will help you understand better where he is coming from.

▌ For the scholar Augustine, this scene of Adam and Eve being chased from the Garden of Eden holds the key to understanding evil in today's world.

Q: Good evening St Augustine, we're here to discuss your theodicy, but first tell us why you chose this subject.

A: Evil appears to surround us and it's dangerous. It hurts you physically but worse, it causes some people to doubt God's existence. Because I know they are completely wrong, I had to work out reasons why evil exists alongside God.

Q: Is it possible God doesn't exist?

A: No. That's totally impossible! God is the one certainty we have. I started my search with the Bible which, as the Word of God, can't be wrong. Looking at your picture above, I can see that you too know the answer to the problem of evil lies in the Book of Genesis. There it says God created the universe and everything in it.

Q: So he created evil then?

A: Certainly not! A perfect being like God couldn't create evil. It's logically impossible. Think about it another way. If a perfect God created everything in existence then it is impossible for evil to exist.

Q: But we know evil exists as sure as …

A: No. You think evil is present but you have got it wrong. Evil is not a substance, it's an absence. It is the absence of goodness. If you are ill, that means you aren't in good health, doesn't it?

Q: But what about if somebody has thumped me? The hurt is real enough!

A: Quite so. That pain has resulted from the absence of kind feelings. Remember the inconsistent triad? Well think about it logically. We know God is good, we know God is omniscient, yet we see evil in the world. So it must follow that the inconsistency lies with our concept of evil. Evil is not a substance, it is a **privation**.

Q: Where does it come from? That's supposing you can say 'it' for something that doesn't exist!

A: Your answer is in the picture. God created a perfect world. Adam and Eve were made in God's likeness and lived in harmony with God and nature in the Garden of Eden.

Q: So what went wrong?

A: The Fall of Man. Adam and Eve disobeyed God and that created sin, or call it evil. Because God is omniscient he knew this would happen. Just as he had foreseen that dispute between the angels which led to Satan being kicked out of heaven for his arrogance.

Q: Couldn't God stop it? I thought he was omnipotent.

A: Of course he could, but a perfect creation isn't one with robots! God knew this would happen and made plans for it.

Q: Hang on, if God didn't cause the evil, who did?

A: They did. The first humans. God gave the angels and humans he created the free will to choose whether to love and obey him or not.

Q: That's risky.

A: But without free will God's creation would be merely mechanical. No, for creation to be truly good, God's creatures must be free to choose. You value a relationship more when a person chooses to love you rather than love someone else?

Q: Yes. But what if people choose the wrong thing?

A: They punish themselves just as Adam and Eve did. When they turned away from good they had to leave Eden. Adam and Eve had destroyed God's natural order and that created natural evil.

Q: Yes but it was all in the past. What's it got to do with us today?

A: We all descended from Adam and Eve so we inherit their guilt. Some humans today turn away from God and evil flourishes. But this is a loving God, who sent his Son Jesus Christ to save us. Jesus' sacrifice paid for Adam and Eve's original sin so humans who want to, can get close to God once more.

Q: Thank you.

KEY WORD

Privation means the absence, or a lack, of something. In this case it is the lack of goodness.

ACTIVITY

Draw a flow diagram showing how the Augustinian Theodicy works or describe it. Include the key terms privation, Fall of Man and free will.

ACTIVITY

A01 skills

Make up two questions to challenge Augustine's theodicy.

ACTIVITY

Using Augustine's theory of evil as a privation rather than existing in its own right, define blindness, earthquake, torture and famine. Do you think the concept of evil as a privation works?

FOR DEBATE

God is not responsible for evil.

4.3 Irenaeus' Theodicy

In this topic you will study Irenaeus' explanation of the problem of evil and then consider the strengths and weaknesses of the different arguments.

Irenaeus' interpretation of Genesis

Irenaeus (c130–202) lived some two hundred years before Augustine. He too began his argument from a position of belief in God and acceptance of the Book of Genesis. He focused on the creation story in Genesis 1 and particularly this quotation.

> Then God said,
> 'And now we will make human beings; they will be like us and resemble us.'
> Genesis 1:26

Irenaeus identified two parts in this quotation. 'Like us' he took to mean God created people with intelligence, morality and a personality. 'Resemble us' he interpreted as meaning people's souls would grow spiritually until they resembled the nature of God. Since humanity needs to develop, it follows that the first humans God created were immature beings, whose soul would develop as those humans learned things.

Free will

Irenaeus believed God gave people free will because it is through making our own mistakes in life we learn about right and wrong. Since free will entails having a choice between good and evil, then evil must exist for us to exercise our choice. When we choose the evil path, it causes moral evil. Nevertheless Irenaeus argued, free will is an essential part of what it means to be human. If an omnipotent God removed evil from the world, he would also remove our humanity and reduce us to mere robots. Irenaeus interpreted Adam and Eve's expulsion from the Garden of Eden as the result of God's immature people exercising free will and making a mistake.

■ What would Irenaeus have said was the purpose of the terrible floods of 2007?

MAKING LINKS

Can you see where Darwin's Theory of Evolution has echoes in Irenaeus' Theodicy?

Pages 56–57 may help you.

ACTIVITY   A02 skills

Script an interview with Irenaeus about his theodicy along the lines of the one with Augustine on pages 72–73.

Evil is necessary

The modern philosopher, John Hick developed Irenaeus' argument further, explaining that evil and suffering were necessary for human development because qualities such as kindness and compassion can grow out of suffering. He believes that soul-making may continue in the next world and natural evil such as earthquakes and famine are God-given opportunities for people to develop their spiritual side. Irenaeus was convinced that eventually everybody's soul would develop sufficiently for them to enter heaven.

Some strengths and weaknesses of Irenaeus' Theodicy

- He offers an explanation for suffering as well as natural and moral evil.

- He argues that the end justifies the means, but some people may question how much suffering is necessary to teach a lesson.

- Some people suffer considerably more than others. Why has God singled them out especially?

- Would a loving God use evil?

- Irenaeus doesn't satisfactorily explain why God couldn't create humans to be morally perfect.

- The concept of humans progressively improving fits in with theories of evolution.

The idea that everyone will eventually go to heaven seems unfair. If everyone is destined to land up in heaven what's the point of the exercise? Where is free choice for those people who don't want to go to heaven?

Some strengths and weaknesses of Augustine's Theodicy

- The concept of evil being a privation yet not part of God's creation is illogical.

- People who are suffering may not find this theodicy a convincing explanation when their pain is very real.

- Evil appears from nowhere.

- The idea that evil can arise when people exercise free will fits with what we see around us.

- If the world began as perfect, where could Adam and Eve find out about evil? Did their understanding of evil come from God?

- Augustine's idea that humans began as perfect, then fell from grace, goes the opposite way to the Theory of Evolution.

- Where did Hell and Satan come from? Were they created by a loving God?

You might have noticed that neither theologian approached the problem of evil from the direction that the existence of evil may prove God does not exist. As convinced believers this is not surprising but is, of course, a weakness in their arguments.

4.4 Religion and Science – any problem?

In this topic you will examine the perceived conflict between religion and science.

KEY WORD

Creationism is an acceptance of the Genesis account of the creation of the universe as factual truth.

March 9 2002

Scandal of school teaching Bible stories as science

CRITICS WERE UP in arms about reports that Emmanuel College, Gateshead, a state-funded secondary, was teaching anti-evolutionary theories. The school, part of the Vardy Foundation, was sponsored by Sir Peter Vardy, an evangelical Christian who donated £2 million towards its construction.

In science lessons, pupils are taught the Genesis account of God creating the world in six days alongside the Darwinian theory of evolution. Sir Peter Vardy said, 'We present them both. One is a theory, the other is a faith position. It is up to the children. We give them an all-round education so both are presented to the students.'

Oxford professor, Richard Dawkins, attacked the school's science teaching saying: 'To call evolution a faith position equated with **creationism** is educational debauchery. It is teaching something that is utter nonsense. Evolution is supported by mountains of scientific evidence. These children are being deliberately and wantonly misled.'

According to the National Curriculum, schools must teach evolution but are free to teach other theories as well. The school's head, Nigel McQuoid, said that it was 'fascist' to say that schools must not consider creationist theories; whilst Sir Peter Vardy said, 'All we are saying is that it's up to children to make their own minds up. I haven't had any complaints … The parents are happy, the students and teachers are happy; we have them standing in queues waiting to get in.'

Another state school in London run by the Seventh Day Adventists also teaches creationism alongside Darwinism. Their director of education explained that 'just like other schools we also explain the concept of evolution. Everyone is free to have their view. What I find amazing is the intolerance and arrogance of people who say you can only believe in evolution and that's all you can teach.'

One Ofsted inspector said, 'The way science works is that you set up a hypothesis and test it and see if it is validated. There is absolutely no concrete evidence to prove evolution.'

▌ (Based on articles in *The Guardian* 9/3/02 and 19/3/02 © Guardian News and Media Limited)

'*People want confrontation,*' said physical biochemist and Anglican priest, Dr Arthur Peacocke, '*religion versus science is good copy.*' What is most surprising is that it's a debate that has raged for more than a hundred years with supporters just as equally split today. It is a surprise because it is often assumed that modern science has defeated religion with facts, when in fact science has not produced any definitive answers to big questions such as: How did we get here? Why are we here? A survey of 2,000 people by the BBC in 2007 asked people what best described their view of the origin and development of life: 22% chose creationism; 17% chose Intelligent Design; 48% opted for the Theory of Evolution and the rest did not know.

A twenty-first century American survey asked parents what their children should be taught about the origins of the world in science lessons. Half said they felt evolution was unproven and the majority wanted the Genesis account of God creating the world taught to their children. Two-thirds of those questioned had no problem accepting Biblical stories of creation alongside scientific accounts of creation.

The big questions – how we got here and why we are here – have occupied philosophers and theologians for centuries. Science as a separate discipline is the newcomer. Each employs a different approach. As someone once said: Religion asks why and science asks how.

Given these different approaches there are likely to be different answers and those answers may not be incompatible.

MAKING LINKS

A01 skills

Remind yourself of Aristotle's Prime Mover and the Teleological argument (see pages 22–23). What was the reasoned philosophical explanation of creation?

Remind yourself of the Judaeo-Christian explanation for creation (see pages 30–31). How is this explanation arrived at?

FURTHER RESEARCH

A01 skills

Find out what the Scopes Monkey Trial was, then give a presentation to the group explaining the significance of this famous case.

STRETCH & CHALLENGE

A01+A02 Skills

Investigate one newspaper's assertion that amongst present-day members of the Royal Society many biologists are atheists, whilst many astronomers and physicists are theists. Why might that be?

ACTIVITY

A01 skills

Find out what is meant by Intelligent Design. How does that differ from creationism?

Challenges to religious belief

4.5 The qualities of God

In this topic you will revise your knowledge of evil and your knowledge of the qualities of God.

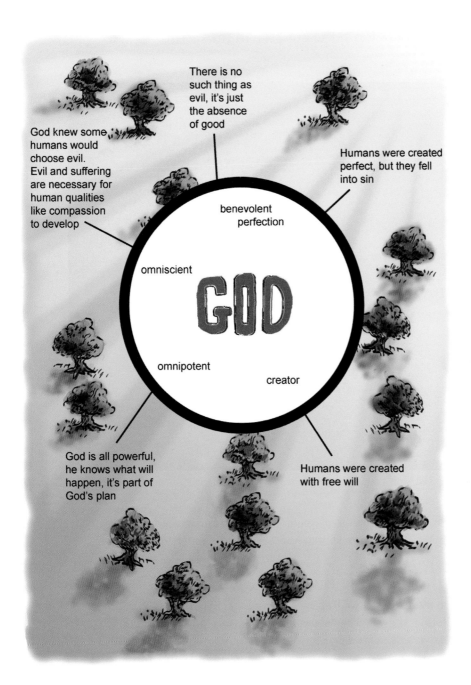

There is no such thing as evil, it's just the absence of good

God knew some humans would choose evil. Evil and suffering are necessary for human qualities like compassion to develop

Humans were created perfect, but they fell into sin

benevolent perfection

omniscient

GOD

omnipotent

creator

God is all powerful, he knows what will happen, it's part of God's plan

Humans were created with free will

ACTIVITY

A01
skills

Prepare material for a webpage on one of the arguments that woud help a student revising this topic for an exam. This could either take the form of further explanation of the argument or an FAQ section.

Challenges to religious belief

4.6 Creation

In this topic you will compare ideas held by theologians and scientists about the creation of the world.

ACTIVITY A01 skills

Consider which, if any, of the philosophical arguments you have studied could accept the Big Bang theory as the mechanism for the start of the world?

ACTIVITY A01+A02 Skills

'In the beginning, when God created the universe, the earth was formless and desolate. The raging ocean that covered everything was engulfed in total darkness, and the power of God was moving over the water.'

(Genesis 1:1–2)

Analyse this statement carefully then explain what it is saying about God's role and what pre-existed. In your opinion is the Big Bang theory compatible or incompatible with this?

MAKING LINKS

Remind yourself of the work on God as *creatio ex nihilo* on pages 30–31. Do you think that belief is compatible with the Big Bang theory or not?

▌ Red Shift is scientific evidence for the Big Bang.

Scientists and theologians agree the earth must have come into being at some point. They disagree about how and why it happened.

The Big Bang theory

In the 1920s, Edwin Hubble observed that light from stars became redder the further they travelled away from the earth. From this he deduced that the universe is expanding outwards and, by measuring the red shift, he calculated the speed they were travelling and the date when this movement must have begun. Its start was nicknamed 'the Big Bang' and postulates a cosmic explosion of enormous energy and heat from which all matter was formed.

Stephen Hawking said:

> *An expanding universe does not preclude a creator, but it does place limits on when he might have carried out his job.*

Theological explanations for the creation of the world

The opening of the Bible supplies theologians with material to help them understand creation and they interpret the Genesis story in a variety of ways.

Creationists believe the Bible gives a factual account of God's creation of the world in six days. Creationism came to the fore in the nineteenth century in the face of Darwinism and today has a particularly strong following in America and amongst some evangelical Christians in Britain.

For other theologians, creation is an ongoing process in which God plays a part. This view does not negate God's role at the start of creation, but places greater emphasis on God's role in the daily life of humans. For these theologians, the Genesis story is not a literal account of creation but a story designed to help people understand their relationship with God and the natural world. The scientific account of the Big Bang does explain the method of creation, though not the reason.

Rev. Dr John Polkinghorne was professor of Mathematical Physics at Cambridge for twenty-five years before he became an Anglican minister. He wrote:

> *I want to say that the physical universe as we experience it and know it, originated in the fiery explosion of the big bang. But that doesn't to my mind, stop me also saying that God created the world. And by that I don't mean that He lit the blue touch paper that started the big bang, but that God is the one who upholds the world and keeps it in being. I want to say that for two reasons. One is that it explains to me the rational order and beauty of the universe, which is very striking for a scientist. Also it explains a very deep human intuition – which is there, despite all the terrible things which happen in the world – the intuition of hope, that there is a meaning and purpose in what's going on. It is not all just a tale told by an idiot. I think that that's a very profound understanding that we have, and I think that God being the Creator of the world is the ground of that hope.*

Interestingly astronomer Professor Fred Hoyle, an atheist, admitted he found it difficult to explain some of his discoveries. 'Would you not say to yourself, "Some super-calculating intellect must have designed the properties of the carbon atom, otherwise the chance of my finding such an atom through the blind forces of nature would be utterly minuscule." Of course you would.' He also said that he thought the chances of even a single cell emerging by random chance was as likely as a tornado sweeping through a junk yard and assembling a Boeing 747.

Professor Richard Dawkins, the evolutionary biologist, challenges all religious accounts of creation. He has said:

> *Evolution is not a faith position. Like the 'theory' the earth is round and not flat, evolution is supported by mountains of scientific evidence, accepted by informed scientists and church people from the Pope on.*

FOR DEBATE A02 skills

Teaching the theory of Intelligent Design as part of a science lesson is no more valid than teaching alchemy in a Chemistry lesson.

ACTIVITY 4.4

Write a paper for the governors of a school where the teaching of scientific theories and Creationism is an issue. Ensure that you report scientific, philosophical and theological beliefs fully and fairly. A01 skills

FURTHER RESEARCH A01 skills

Find out what the 'Goldilocks theory' is. Would it offer support to scientists or theologians?

4.7 Evolution

In this topic you will compare the views of some theologians with some scientists on the subject of life on earth.

Today biology textbooks in Alabama, USA, must carry this statement on the outside:

> *This book may discuss Evolution, a controversial theory some scientists give as an explanation for the origin of living things, such as plants, animals and humans. No human was present when life first appeared on earth, therefore any statement about life's origins should be treated as theory, not fact.*

The statement from the Alabama biology textbooks, which caused uproar when it first appeared, sums up the dilemma perfectly. What is surprising is that the controversy should surface at the end of the twentieth century and continue today, rather than belong in the nineteenth century.

Darwin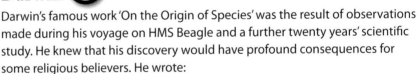

Darwin's famous work 'On the Origin of Species' was the result of observations made during his voyage on HMS Beagle and a further twenty years' scientific study. He knew that his discovery would have profound consequences for some religious believers. He wrote:

> *I am almost convinced (quite contrary to the opinion I started with) that species are not (it is like confessing to a murder) **immutable**.*

Darwin's assertion that different species had evolved from one common ancestor, challenged the Church's teaching that God created each species of animals and designed humans to be like himself.

Darwin's second point was that the changes in the species occurred through 'natural selection' with only those species who were well adapted to their environment surviving to breed and pass their characteristics on to the next generation. This conflicted with the account in Genesis of every being created for a special purpose.

The theory of Natural Selection presented some theologians with a challenge because the Genesis story showed God creating every life for a purpose in his creation. Darwin, however, was not arguing for totally random creation. The process he describes has a cause but it lacks a controlling intelligence or a sense of purpose. As Mill had observed, it is a wasteful and cruel world, where species die out or are killed. There is no place in Darwin's world for a God who is concerned about the welfare or suffering of his creation.

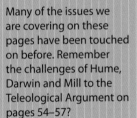

FOR DEBATE **A02** *skills*

The statement on the right is perfectly true. All British biology textbooks should carry the same warning in the interests of fairness.

MAKING LINKS

Many of the issues we are covering on these pages have been touched on before. Remember the challenges of Hume, Darwin and Mill to the Teleological Argument on pages 54–57?

KEY WORD

Immutable means unchanged since creation.

ACTIVITY **A01** *skills*

Make a leaflet to help you revise the scientific challenge to religion.

4.3

Where does this leave believers?

As the Alabama textbook sticker showed, some believers are reluctant to accept Darwin's Theory of Evolution because it is 'a theory'. Other modern theologians have no difficulty understanding evolution as part of God's method.

> *Within the continuities of these processes there arises homo sapiens, a being who is undoubtedly a product of the natural process and yet has the mental capacity to know the process and to know that he or she knows – thereby evidencing an extraordinary distance from even the most intelligent primate or porpoise.*
>
> Rev Arthur Peacocke, Oxford physical biochemist and Anglican priest
>
> *A lot of people see evolution and believing in God as somehow in tension or incompatible, whereas my thinking has been coming round to the idea that God has to use evolution in order to create intelligent life.*
>
> Denis Alexander, Cambridge geneticist
>
> *God makes things to make themselves,*
>
> Rev Arthur Peacocke

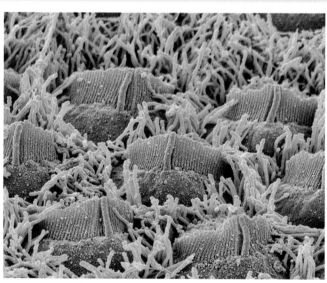

▌ Behe says, *'No one at all can give a detailed account of how the cilium or any complex biochemical process might have developed in a Darwinian fashion. But we are here. All these things got here somehow; if not a Darwinian fashion, then how?'*

In 1996 Professor Michael Behe launched an academic attack on Darwinism. He argued that life at a molecular level is so complex it could not have come about by small incremental changes. Everything has to function at the same time; it would not work if parts only evolved gradually. Behe says Darwin has no explanation for such life. From that Behe constructs his argument that **irreducible complexity** is best accounted for by **Intelligent Design**; such irreducible complexity exists in living cells. The best explanation for such life is an Intelligent Designer. That is God.

ACTIVITY A01+A02 Skills

Biology is the field where God really did his best work. In a way, Darwin pulled a much bigger rug out from under God's feet than physics has ever done.

(Professor Richard Dawkins, a zoologist and Oxford professor, who is an atheist.)

Explain Dawkins' point. How might a theologian respond?

STRETCH & CHALLENGE A01 skills

Investigate Professor Dawkins' arguments further in his books *The God Delusion* or *The Blind Watchmaker*. Report your findings to the group.

ACTIVITY A01+A02 Skills

Explain Behe's point and give an opposing viewpoint. 4.5

KEY WORD

Irreducible complexity: the idea that some biological organisms are too complex to evolve without the help of an unevolved intelligence.

Intelligent Design: the idea that the universe must have a designer rather than being the result of change or undirected natural processes.

ExamCafé
Relax, refresh, result!

Relax and prepare

The challenges to religious belief

Jess

When I revise I feel that I learn topics well but I don't seem to do well on exam questions. I look at it and think, how can I get 25 marks on this? I particularly struggled to get to grips with the problem of evil.

Several students have offered Jess their advice. Some of the posted comments are more useful than others. What further advice could you give to help Jess?

Rhiannon

Jess, one thing I often do is to try to imagine I am someone reading this who hasn't studied the subject. Of course, my examiner will know the subject (at least I hope so!). I guess that I want my imaginary reader to understand what I'm writing.

This means that each point becomes two or three sentences rather than one. Otherwise they won't know what I'm getting at. This helps to 'explain' rather than just say what something is. Hope this helps.

Stephen

I have always believed in keeping things short and to the point. If you can answer the question in 15 minutes, that leaves you more time for other questions. I saved time on all the questions in the end and finished a 1½ hour exam in well under the hour. As I looked at everyone else writing, I wondered if I had got it all wrong. When results day came, I *knew* I'd got it wrong. Thank goodness for re-sits!'

Laura

During my Philosophy of Religion exam I realised when I was writing my first answer that although I'd studied the problem of evil, I'd never really thought about what my views were. I'm going to look at other topics and work out what I believe before I do any more exams.

Sian

One thing I had to do was to find a way of remembering the differences between Augustine and Irenaeus. Augustine looks backwards to what went wrong, Irenaeus looks forward to the ultimate good that will be done by suffering.

Think about the issues as you study them. For example, on this current topic, what is your view? Do you think that the existence of evil and suffering makes it unlikely/impossible for God to exist, or does one of the theodicies work?

A Level Religious Studies is not just about the exam. It can develop your knowledge and understanding of different viewpoints and help you to develop ideas of your own. If you do this, it will actually benefit your examination performance, particularly on part b) questions. You won't need to spend five minutes scratching your head wondering what you believe about the topic.

Engage with the topic and enjoy working out your ideas before the exam. Here are a few possible ideas of what you could argue on the problem of evil.

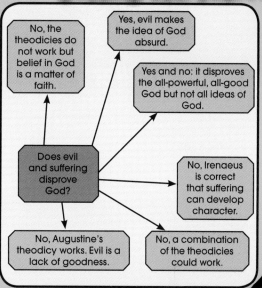

No, the theodicies do not work but belief in God is a matter of faith.

Yes, evil makes the idea of God absurd.

Yes and no: it disproves the all-powerful, all-good God but not all ideas of God.

Does evil and suffering disprove God?

No, Irenaeus is correct that suffering can develop character.

No, Augustine's theodicy works. Evil is a lack of goodness.

No, a combination of the theodicies could work.

Refresh your memory

Revision checklist for the challenges to religious belief

In order to do well on these topics you will need to:

▷ Be able to explain clearly the problem of evil; understand the concepts of natural evil and moral evil.

▷ Understand the theodicy of Augustine; his views on the origin of evil, free will and the responsibility of God.

▷ Critically discuss the theodicy of Augustine.

▷ Understand the theodicy of Irenaeus; his views on the origin of evil, free will and the responsibility of God.

▷ Critically discuss the theodicy of Irenaeus.

▷ Be able to compare and contrast the two theodicies.

▷ Understand the different views on the origin of the universe.

▷ Explain the views of Darwin and how they have been developed in recent times.

▷ Understand the ideas of creationism and the Big Bang theory.

▷ Explain recent developments such as intelligent design and irreducible complexity.

▷ Be able to assess the above theories and thinkers.

Remember that in your final AS exam you will be answering two-part questions. Part a) questions are testing your knowledge and understanding of the material that you have studied. Part b) questions are testing your ability to evaluate ideas.

Get the result!

Sample answers

Exam question

(a) Explain the Augustinian theodicy. (25 marks)

Examiner says

As an examiner marking Stephen's answer I have a dilemma. What he has written is brief but accurate. Is he clever but lazy, and actually knows far more than he has written? Maybe he is a weak student who has a good memory, perhaps he has remembered this but understands none of it! The point is that if he doesn't write it down, it cannot be marked. The answer does include the main points, but Stephen has not written anything else that 'shows understanding of them'; therefore he can only be awarded a limited mark.

Stephen's answer

Augustine believed that God is perfect and created a perfect world. God made everything except evil. Evil is not a substance in its own right. It is merely the absence (or privation) of good. Evil comes when the angels and first human beings deliberately choose to turn away from God. This sin gets passed down because everyone was present in Adam's loins. Therefore everyone deserves to be punished.

Natural evil comes about because humans destroyed the natural order. The first human beings were the representatives of creation and they are the reason why the created order falls. God saves some people through their acceptance of Christ. This shows that he is merciful as well as just and hence explains why God is justified in allowing evil.

Stephen has certainly covered most of Augustine's points. Can you use his cues to construct your own answer to the question? How would your answer have done? Ask your teacher if you are not sure.

Exam question

(b) 'There is too much evil in the world to believe the argument in the theodicies.' Discuss. (10 marks)

Laura's original answer

I think this is true, it is difficult to believe in a God that allows things such as the Holocaust and earthquakes. There are lots of things on the news each night where people suffer or evil occurs. A lot of this evil is caused directly by humans. God gave us free will and it is our fault that much of the evil is in the world, so it's unfair to blame God.

Suffering can't just be the result of human free will. There is natural evil such as earthquakes and volcanoes. These cause lots of suffering but no humans are involved and none of the theodicies say anything about natural evil. Irenaeus has an answer to the problem of evil, he argues that suffering can develop our character and make us better people, just as exercise develops our bodies. This is a good idea so maybe the theodicies can work.

Laura's improved answer

It could be argued that the existence of evil and suffering is a strong argument against belief in God. There is certainly a lot of suffering that seems pointless. We see on the TV news each night images of earthquakes and war. In recent history we have had the attack on the Twin Towers and the Holocaust. These events cause many to question the existence of God. However, if the issue is analysed further, we may note that much of the evil and suffering in the world is the direct result of human free will. Augustine argued that evil cannot be God's responsibility but must come from humans misusing their free will. Augustine's theodicy is correct in suggesting that human action causes much suffering, but has been criticised by some who think it relies on a literal reading of the Bible.

One area where Augustine's explanation is lacking is in the area of natural evil. This is where Irenaeus' theodicy can be seen to be better. Irenaeus is quite correct to suggest that difficulties that we face in life can make us stronger as people. In the same way that exercise can make us stronger physically, so suffering may have a helpful effect on our character. Irenaeus argues that the world has to be a suitable environment for character development. It has to be a little tough. Hick refers to this as the vale of soul making. Therefore despite the vast amounts of suffering in the world, it is still possible to accept the theodicies.

Examiner says

Laura has contradicted herself here. Both points she makes are relevant but I'm not sure which her real view is. This could have read coherently if the second viewpoint had been introduced with 'However...' or 'Others may argue...' or some similar phrase.

Examiner says

A little more detail and a lot more clarity of argument. Augustine is named and considered rather than just hinted at.

Examiner says

Laura changes her mind twice more. Look at the mark scheme. It is debatable whether there is successful analysis here. If there is, I'm having to put the pieces of the argument together myself. In the end it's not very successful. There is also a factual error – can you spot it?

Examiner says

First sentence links to previous paragraph. Irenaeus is introduced; his argument is explained and considered well. The essay actually concludes whereas the first attempt ground to a halt. Perhaps could have included more of a range of material for even better marks.

ExamCafé
Relax, refresh, result!

Relax and prepare

You are the judge

When you answer the evaluation questions on the philosophy paper, it may be helpful to think of yourself as judge in a courtroom presenting your ruling. You will need to sum up and respond to the prosecution evidence (the case against the argument or idea) and consider the defence evidence (the case in defence of the argument) before announcing your verdict (conclusion).

You could use a writing frame like the one below. Remember, you can invert it if you happen to like the argument that you are assessing (then the prosecution could be arguing for an idea and the defence arguing against it).

_____'s argument has a number of key weaknesses.

Firstly _____. (You will need to explain the weakness and suggest a counterargument if you are aware of one.)

Secondly, a further weakness is found in _____. (Do the same again.)

Thirdly, another philosopher called _____ also criticises the concept by arguing that _____. (Explain as before.)

However, supporters of the _____ argument would point to its key strengths. Firstly, _____ (Explain in full.). A second argument in favour would be _____. (Explain again.)

In conclusion, it can be seen that the _____ argument has several key weaknesses and it is difficult to see how the argument can succeed given these issues.

(Give your summary or 'ruling' in 'the third person': i.e. say 'It can be seen that...' rather than 'I think that...' – makes it more official.)

Examiner's tip

Remember, for a good part b) answer, there has to be 'successful and _clear_ analysis.' Using a structure similar to the one above will help bring clarity to the argument that you are presenting.

Refresh your memory

This is a timeline of philosophers; you will be able to see which topic you have met them in.

BCE

Jewish exile in Babylon 597BCE
Old Testament completed by 400–300BCE
Plato (428–347BCE): The Cave and the Forms
Aristotle (384–322BCE): The Causes and the Prime Mover

Jesus lives and New Testament completed by c.140CE

Irenaeus (c.130–c.205): Problem of Evil: suffering builds character

Augustine of Hippo (354–430): Problem of Evil: suffering comes from Adam and Eve
Boethius (480–524)

Anselm (1033–1109): The Ontological Argument: two forms
Gaunilo: Criticises the Ontological Argument: perfect island
Aquinas (c.1225–1274): Teleological Argument: order and regularity. Cosmological Argument: motion, causation, contingency

Descartes (1596–1650): The Ontological Argument: triangles
Hume (1711–1776): Criticises the Cosmological Argument. Criticises the Teleological Argument
Paley (1743–1805): The Teleological Argument: the watch
Kant (1724–1804): Criticises the Ontological Argument: existence is not a predicate. Presents a Moral Argument for God
Mill (1806–1873): Criticises the Teleological Argument: evil in world
Darwin (1809–1882): Religion and Science: evolution. Criticises the Teleological Argument
Freud (1856–1939): Criticises the Moral Argument
Russell: (1872–1970): Critic of the Cosmological Argument.
Copleston (1907–1994): Modern defender of Cosmological Argument
Ayer (1910–1989)
Polkinghorne (1930–): Religion and Science: theistic evolution
Plantinga (1932–)
Phillips (1934–2006)
Swinburne (1934–): Modern Supporter of the Teleological Argument
Dawkins (1941–): Religion and Science: modern supporter of Darwin
Behe (1952–): Religion and Science: Intelligent Design

Present day

This chart is arranged by thinkers. Why not create your own chart that is arranged by topic? They could be simple spider diagrams or full ideas maps.

Get the result!

Language of the exam:

Explain what you mean by 'explain'

Suppose you were asked to explain how football was played, or even how you came to be at college/school this morning.

- If you write a brief paragraph to the effect of 'two teams kick the ball into nets and the one who does it the most times wins' or 'I woke up, caught the bus and came to class', you have given an explanation but you haven't given the sort of detail that an intelligent and thoughtful questioner would want. Your RS examiner is looking for **depth**. Explain *is not the same as* 'give a brief account'.

- If you were to explain that football is one of many ball games and go on speak at length about cricket, or you were to discuss your breakfast in minute detail, you are explaining but you are not explaining what you are *asked* to explain. You must **focus** on the question *that is asked*.

- If you were to launch into a discussion of the significance of football in modern society or were to debate the legality of your school or college daring to suggest that you attend lessons, you are not explaining. You should avoid the temptation to do part b) type discussion when you should be **explaining**.

Sample answers

Exam question

(a) Explain the Platonic concept of 'Forms' (25 marks)

Mai Li's answer

Plato's concept of the Forms derives from the idea that the physical world in which we live is a pale reflection of the truth. Every concept, such as beauty, and every object, such as a tree, has a Form, existing in the world of the Forms infinitely more perfect than its particular in the world of the senses.

Examiner says

So far, so good. Key ideas introduced. Mai Li now needs to explain some of these ideas in detail.

Examiner says

Mai Li has added that Forms are like ideals and has briefly mentioned the Form of the Good. However, her examples repeat what has been said earlier and add no depth to the overall answer

The world of the Forms exists outside our senses and contains the Forms or ideals for every object or particular we encounter in this world of the senses. For example, for every beauty we encounter through our senses, beauty has a Form, the most pure and perfect form of beauty. Plato's concept also had a certain hierarchy. The Form of the Good is the most important Form. It is the Form of the Forms.

This is where holes start to appear in Plato's teachings. If everything has an ideal then maybe there is an ideal of the ideal, and so on. Also Aristotle questioned the Form of the Good. Goodness is goodness and can't be more good by making it infinite.

Examiner says

This is poor technique. This material is more appropriate in part b). There are no AO1 marks here and for the purposes of marking I ignore this paragraph and award marks based on the first two paragraphs. The mark scheme asks for 'good understanding' and 'good selection of material'; this answer isn't quite there.

Mai Li's improved answer

Plato was a pupil of the previous philosopher Socrates. He taught and learnt through question and answer methods, known as dialectic methods.

Examiner says

Interesting background information. No actual marks here but serves as a brief introduction.

Plato believed that there were two worlds, the material world we live in and the world of Forms. He also said that there are two types of knowledge, empirical, knowledge gained through the senses and true knowledge, which was gained a priori through reason. It is this knowledge that the philosopher has by escaping the cave and looking at the Forms.

Plato believed that the world of the Forms was a perfect and unchanging world. Previous philosophers had said that the world we live in was always changing. Plato agreed but believed that there was a realm that was unchanging. The Forms are eternal and unchanging. The perfect idea of beauty remains the same despite the fact that particular examples of beauty, e.g. a model, will change over time. The Forms are also perfect. Even a beautiful model will have some blemishes hidden away, but the perfect Form of beauty is just that — perfect. Forms are ideals or categories; they are what certain things (particulars) have in common. How do we recognise that an object is a chair despite the fact that it is completely different to all other chairs we have seen? Because it possesses the Form of the chair.

Get the result!

Examiner says

Super! Look at the mark scheme. There is a lot of high level information here. Mai Li has shown that she understands and can use technical terms. This answer is likely to get a high grade.

Plato suggested that the most important Form had to be the Form of the Good. This is represented by the sun in the analogy of the cave. There is a hierarchy of Forms with goodness at the top, then universal qualities such as beauty and justice then there were forms of ordinary things such as cats, chairs and table. Plato argued that the Form of the Good was the most important Form because of its link to ethics. We will be good if we know what goodness is. Hence the concept of Forms is crucial to Plato's ideas.

Mai Li

Hot tips

I now know what it means when the exam asks you to explain something. To be honest, the first time around, I ran out of stuff to say about Forms and started rambling.

Exam question

(a) To what extent is it true to say that the Forms teach us nothing about the physical world? (10 marks)

Fran's answer

Some would say that Plato's theory of the Forms is of little use in understanding the physical world. They would say this because he doesn't actually have any proof that another realm exists. If there is a perfect Form of everything, then is there a perfect Form of bacteria, for instance? Bacteria seem to have little purpose, why would bacteria need a Form? This would cause people to question the concept of the Forms. There would also have to be a Form of everything, including the television before it was invented. Forms may also be very specific or very vague. Is there just one Form of the dog or are there many Forms: the Form of the brown haired spaniel, the male greyhound, etc? Religious people might agree with the Forms as they teach us that physical things are not as important as the spiritual. The weaknesses of the Forms outweigh the strengths, so the Forms are unlikely to be true.

Fran's improved answer

Plato's Forms can be seen to be of little use in understanding the physical world. However, Plato would not see this as a problem. He argues that the truth is not to be found in this world. The Forms, found in the real world, contain knowledge. This world is of little consequence to him and he is not interested in discovering scientific knowledge when there are eternal truths of mathematics and the Forms.

Plato's Forms are seen by many as being too remote and too abstract to help us understand the world. It may be that there is no such thing as the Forms and that the 'Form' is just a convenient label for things that we recognise as similar to each other. Wittgenstein calls this 'family' resemblance. Each one looks a little like each of the others but there is no one characteristic that is shared by others.

However, it can be argued that the Forms may help us understand the world around us. When we see something beautiful, Plato believes that we are recognising the Form of beauty present to some degree in that particular. This enables us to have a clear standard as to what is beautiful and good. In ethical dilemmas in this world, Plato's Forms, if true, would enable us to have a definite black and white answer. Ultimately, for most people this is irrelevant as there seems little reason to think that there are such things as Forms.

Examiner says

At first glance a reasonable structure and an attempt to argue both sides, giving strengths and weaknesses. But look again at the question. Fran is being asked whether the Forms teach us anything about the physical world, she is not being asked whether they are coherent. Any analysis is implied and not clear.

Examiner says

Don't worry if you haven't looked at Wittgenstein, there are plenty of other arguments that can be used. Remember, your examiners are not looking for specific philosophers (unless they are mentioned in the question), so any valid material will be credited.

Examiner says

You might feel this is brave but Fran is quite right. If the statement in the question appears odd or over-simplistic, then say so and say why. Don't be afraid to take the question apart if need be.

Examiner says

The answer is now two sided and a conclusion is given which clearly sums up Fran's view. This answer is now improved, perhaps needing a greater 'range of evidence' for full marks.

Fran

Hot tips

I had learned the strengths and weaknesses of the Forms and when I saw the question I just went for it. It wasn't until it was marked that I even considered that I'd done badly. I was shocked, but now I know to read the question carefully rather than just think they want me to assess the topic.

Ethical theories

Do you have to look outside yourself to a **higher power** in order to know what is right and wrong? Or does everybody **instinctively** know right from wrong?

In this chapter you will learn:

- about what is meant by absolutist and relativist morality and objective and subjective morality

- what Aquinas meant by Natural Law and the strengths and weaknesses of that ethical theory

- how Kant developed his view of ethics and the strengths and weaknesses of that ethical theory

- what Bentham and Mill meant by Utilitarianism and examine the strengths and weaknesses of this ethical theory

- how Christian ethics has developed and compare it with the other ethical theories you have studied.

Do you have to look outside yourself to a **higher power** in order to know what is right and wrong? Or does everybody **instinctively** know right from wrong?

Ethical theories

5.1 Is it right or is it wrong?

In this topic you will learn the difference between making an ethical decision based on absolutist morality and on relativist morality.

ACTIVITY

Decide whether the girl in the picture's actions were right or wrong.

What have you based your verdict on? If you couldn't decide, why was that?

The girl in the picture, Bekky, is sixteen and lives in a bedsit with five-month-old Josh. Bekky is desperately short of cash because her boyfriend hasn't sent her any money for weeks. The baby keeps crying because he's hungry. The supermarket Bekky stole baby food from made 5.7 million pounds profit last year.

Do you want to change your judgement of Bekky's action?

■ This girl has been arrested for stealing from the supermarket.

KEY WORDS

Absolutist: a rule that is true in all situations.

Relativist: a judgement that depends on the circumstances; there is no universal right or wrong.

Subjective: judgements are based on personal opinion and not on any fixed rules.

Objective: judgements are based on an impartial absolute value system.

Making ethical judgements

Making any ethical judgement about something involves us deciding what is right and what is wrong. To do that we have to have some sort of moral code to measure things against. This immediately raises the question: how do we know what is right and wrong?

Stealing is wrong

Whether or not you took any notice of the sob story about Bekky, stealing is wrong. There are absolutely no two ways about it! We were all taught as children that you can't go around taking things that don't belong to you and every day life has reinforced that rule since. 'Do not steal' is also number eight of the Ten Commandments. What else do you need to tell you stealing is bad?

A moral judgement that relies on a fixed truth like this is **absolutist**. An absolutist rule says some things are basically right, or in this case wrong, no matter what the circumstances: there is no room for manoeuvre. What makes an ethic **deontological** is that it pays no regard to consequences, as the name makes clear, coming from the Greek for duty. Stealing is always wrong. It makes no difference who does it, what the reasons were, what culture they live in or whether it took place hundreds of years ago. Stealing is just one of those things which is universally wrong and everybody knows that even if they don't obey the rules.

Absolutism

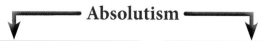

STRENGTHS

- It provides a universal code to measure everything against.
- Absolutism enables us to have a UN Declaration of Human Rights.
- It is easier to apply than relativism.
- Life contains many situations which people instinctively take an absolutist approach to; for example, cruelty to a baby is wrong.

WEAKNESSES

- It doesn't consider different circumstances or cultural attitudes.
- How does anyone know what the absolute morals are?
- It is not concerned with the motive or outcome of an action.

Yes, but be reasonable!

When you read Bekky's problems then weigh her 'crime' up against the amount of money the supermarket makes every day, you might decide she was justified. Her actions might well have saved a baby's life. Surely that is a good outcome and far more important than the £3.65 worth of goods she stole?

A moral judgement that takes circumstances into consideration is **relativist** because it is related to the situation and not to any fixed rules. It also means that no action is good or bad in itself, only by weighing up the whole situation can a judgement be made.

Relativist arguments

Relativist morality has become more popular in the West in recent times. The idea goes back to the ancient Greeks: Protagoras (c480–411 BCE) said nothing was absolutely good or bad, but everybody decides for themselves according to the time and place in which they are living. Others have added religion and culture to the things that help us define what is good and bad.

Supporters of relativism point to the modern clash of cultures between liberal western attitudes and Islamic attitudes towards revealing clothing or cohabitation. The west regards them as a harmless expression of individuality whereas Islamic society considers them wrong because they can lead to immoral behaviour, a breakdown of family life and eventually of society.

Relativism

STRENGTHS

- It is flexible.
- It focuses on people.
- It allows people to take responsibility.

WEAKNESSES

- Judgements are always **subjective**.
- No two people may agree on a judgement.
- Relativism does not allow a society to progress, e.g. some things like genocide have always got to be wrong.
- It is more difficult to apply than absolutism

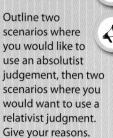

FOR DEBATE A02 skills

Outline two scenarios where you would like to use an absolutist judgement, then two scenarios where you would want to use a relativist judgment. Give your reasons.

STRETCH & CHALLENGE A01 skills

It is possible to make an ethical judgment that is both absolutist and **teleological**. Look at Bekky's story again and suggest an absolutist teleological rule that might be applied in this case.

FOR DEBATE A01+A02 Skills

What did Protagoras mean when he said, 'Man is the measure of all things'? Do you think that is a good arrangement?

KEY WORDS

Deontological: refers to an action that is inherently right or wrong. No account is taken of circumstances or outcome.

Teleological argument: concerned with the purpose or ultimate goal of something.

5.2 The search for a universal law

In this topic you will learn how Aquinas developed the concept of Natural Law from Aristotle's ideas.

The search for a natural law

Those who support an absolutist approach to ethics need to explain where we can get a knowledge of morality from. Do humans have an innate understanding of right and wrong? The Christian philosopher Thomas Aquinas (1224–1274) thought so. He developed the argument for Natural Law from the philosophy of Aristotle (384–322 BCE), who wrote:

> *The natural is that which everywhere is equally valid, and depends not upon being or not being received. That which is natural is unchangeable, and has the same power everywhere, just as fire burns both here and in Persia.*

Aristotelian roots

Aristotle's Theory of Causes is concerned with the essence of something. (See pages 20–21) When considering why an object exists, Aristotle asked, 'How does it happen?'. This question is concerned with the **Efficient Cause** and the answer usually given for an object, like the table on pages 20–21, is that somebody made it.

Aristotle's **Final Cause** refers to the purpose of the object and asked 'What's it for?'. According to Aristotle this cause was the most important because it gave the best explanation of an object. Perfection was only reached when an object did exactly what it was intended to do.

You will notice that the things you worked on in the first Activity section were inanimate objects. What happens if you swap an inanimate object for a human being? We can answer the Efficient Cause fairly easily. We are all here because our parents produced us. But what about the Final Cause? What is the purpose of a human being? Aristotle believed our purpose in life was to seek happiness through general all-round wellbeing, for which he used the Greek word **eudaimonia**. According to his philosophy, everything we do in life is aimed at finding this happiness which enables us to thrive.

The Stoics, a group of Greek philosophers who came after Aristotle, argued that the universe has a basic design and purpose which human morality should work in harmony with. The idea of a morality that follows the natural purpose of life is known as Natural Law.

Aquinas applies Aristotle's Causes to Christianity

Aquinas admired Aristotle's philosophy and unlike some Christian thinkers did not regard its emphasis on reason as a threat to Christianity. If the ability to reason is God-given, how could it be wrong to use it?

ACTIVITY A01 skills

Check your understanding of Aristotle's Efficient Cause and Final Cause by asking and answering the relevant questions of a biro, a shop and a computer.

ACTIVITY A01 skills

Test Aristotle's theory. Write down *'I am sitting in this lesson studying Aristotle in order to…'.* When you have answered it, make that reason the beginning of your next statement. For example, the reason you might have given was to get a good exam result. Then you would start *'I want to get a good exam result in order to…'.* Just keep regressing until you can't get back any further. Was Aristotle right about the purpose of our lives?

FOR DEBATE

Aristotle said that morality should be based on reasoning not emotions. Is that valid?

A02 skills

▮ What would these young people say was the point of this activity?

FURTHER RESEARCH

A01 skills

Research how the Stoics, who included Cicero and Marcus Aurelius, developed the concept of Natural Law. Present your findings as a handout for the group, highlighting the aspects Aquinas developed.

MAKING LINKS

Look at Aquinas' Design Argument on pages 52–53 and find the connection.

ACTIVITY

A01 skills

Work out the meaning of Aquinas' words, from his Summa Contra Gentiles, by breaking his argument down into bullet points and writing them out in your own words, or representing it as a diagram.

When Aquinas looked for an Efficient Cause of the universe, he found God, the power who brought the world into existence.

> *Therefore it is necessary to admit a first efficient cause, to which everyone gives the name of God.*

That was what Aquinas understood from scripture and the order and purpose he observed in the world reflected God's will.

Aquinas' ideas of purpose and perfection

Aquinas said an object achieves its Final Cause or purpose when it does what God intended it to do. For humans, 'made in the image of God', means seeking union with God. That is perfection, but it can only be reached in the afterlife.

> *… some things are so produced by God that, being intelligent, they bear a resemblance to Him and reflect His image: wherefore not only are they directed, but they direct themselves to their appointed end by their own actions. And if in thus directing themselves be they subject to the divine ruling, they are admitted by that divine ruling to the attainment of their last end; but are excluded therefrom if they direct themselves otherwise.*
>
> Summa Contra Gentiles Bk3

How do we know what God intends?

Aquinas believed there is a basic moral law which is divinely inspired that underpins all laws and is there to guide what we do and why we do it. It is that:

> *good is to be done and pursued and evil is to be avoided.*

KEYWORDS

Final Cause: Aristotle used this to mean the purpose of something.

Efficient Cause: Aristotle used this to explain how something happens, the agent which brings something about.

Eudaimonia: the aim of all human activity is to achieve all-round wellbeing.

Ethical theories

5.3 Aquinas and reason

In this topic you will learn how Aquinas used reason to interpret Natural Law.

Unlike many theologians of his day, Aquinas championed the use of reason as Aristotle had. Aquinas believed little was gained from blind faith. Our God-given power of reasoning raises us above other animals and enables us to achieve our ultimate purpose – perfection or union with God.

The use of reason leads a person to arrive at the right course of action when confronted with a moral dilemma. A human can choose to go against reason, but Aquinas said that is 'equivalent to condemning the command of God.'

By employing their power of reason in any situation, a human is putting themselves in touch with Natural Law. This Natural Law, Aquinas believed, was one part of a hierarchical moral code that stretches down to us from God.

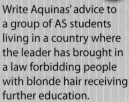

Eternal Law
Eternal Law is the mind of God which humans cannot know. Contained within it are the laws which govern the creation of the universe and control the life cycle of everything in existence. Although humans cannot fully know the Eternal Law, they can occasionally glimpse reflections of it, for example, through scientific knowledge of aspects of the natural world.

Divine Law
Divine Law is the law of God revealed to people through the Bible, which Christians call the 'Word of God'. Jesus Christ, as the Son of God, also brought Divine Law with him and the teachings of the Church transmit Divine Law to people.

Natural Law
Everyone has a natural sense 'that good is to be done and evil avoided' which some call human nature. It is what directs our conscience and if applied with reason to a situation will lead to the right outcome.

Human Law
These are everyday rules that govern our lives, from the legal system at one end right down to notices saying 'Don't walk on the grass'.

▌ Aquinas believed each law depends on the authority of the level above, with God being the ultimate source of all authority.

What hope do non-Christians have?

Anyone who believes in God but is not a Christian would be missing a significant link in the chain of understanding to God. Aquinas was aware of that. Since he believed God created everybody, Christian and non-believer, their ultimate destiny remains the same: fellowship with God. Aquinas believed that God made it possible for all human beings to achieve their ultimate purpose in life by their powers of reasoning alone. However, God chose to reveal himself to humanity through the person of Jesus Christ, whose teachings are transmitted through the Bible. This is extra help for believers striving to reach perfection. Using reason and the Word of God (combining Natural Law and Divine Law) makes it easier for people to reach God. Those who do not believe in Christianity will find it more difficult to achieve their purpose but the way is not closed to them.

Natural Law is the key

Whilst it is possible to leave Christianity out of the route to God, Aquinas did not consider it was possible to leave out Natural Law: this essential God-given part of every person's make-up is what enables us to make moral judgements.

> This is the first precept of law, that 'good is to be done and pursued, and evil is to be avoided'. All other precepts of the natural law are based upon this…
>
> Summa Theologica

Is it real or does it only appear so?

Aquinas believed everyone has the sense of Natural Law within them, which inclines them towards perfection, seeking union with God. Things go wrong when a person becomes misguided in their judgement either because their reasoning is faulty or they have misunderstood the divine law. They may think something is good when it isn't really. It is only an **apparent good**. The AS students who spend all their time clubbing because they think it's good are seeking an apparent good. Reason tells us that some time spent studying gains high level exam results and that is the **real good**.

STRETCH & CHALLENGE A02 skills

Examine the use of the word 'purpose'.

- What do you mean when you use the word?
- What did Aristotle mean by it?
- What did Aquinas understand by the word?
- What is the difference in these usages?

ACTIVITY A01 skills

Unpack the meaning of this quotation from Cicero, one of the Stoics: *'True law is right reason in agreement with nature.'*

Explain how Aquinas interpreted it.

KEY WORDS

Real good: a correct judgement arrived at by the right use of reason along with Natural Law.

Apparent Good: a faulty judgement as a result of the misuse of reason or misunderstanding of Divine Law.

Ethical theories

5.4 Does Aquinas' Natural Law work?

In this topic you will examine how Aquinas understood Natural Law would work in practice and then consider the strengths and weaknesses of this philosophy.

ACTIVITY A01 skills

What would Natural Law say about homosexual acts, masturbation or sex with an infertile partner? Why? How is the Natural Law approach to sexual ethics essentially different from the modern attitude to sex?

ACTIVITY A01 skills

Explain why it is wrong to say 'Natural Law means doing what comes naturally'.

5.2

Aquinas believed the Natural Law philosophy could work in a structured way because we are rational beings who live in a world designed by a rational, purposeful creator. *'A certain order is to be found in those things that are apprehended universally,'* he wrote, and laid out the rules, or precepts, he thought a society would follow.

In order for people to be able to concentrate on Natural Law, Aquinas understood they had to live in a civilised society where they were free to survive and flourish. He set out **Five Primary Precepts** essential for this:

● Preservation of life.

● Reproduction.

● Educating the young.

● Living in a society.

● Worshipping God.

Each of the primary precepts can be developed into **secondary precepts**, which are the practical human rules (see page 100) that govern our daily behaviour. Whilst the primary precepts are set in stone these secondary precepts vary from the law of the land to accepted codes of behaviour within our own family.

Primary Precepts	Possible Secondary Precepts for a society
Preservation of life	● Do not commit suicide ● Do not switch off life-support machines
Reproduction	● Permit IVF and surrogacy ● Contraception is wrong
Educating the young	● Education is free ● Make schooling compulsory
Living in a society	● Build more homes ● Encourage community activities
Worshipping God	● Set one day a week aside for worship ● Hold school assemblies

How do you arrive at the secondary precepts?

Aquinas regarded each precept – primary and secondary – as part of a path towards the ultimate purpose in life. Let's consider the primary precept reproduction, which is obviously essential for the survival of society and indeed the human race. To arrive at the secondary precepts you have to reason what would be an essential route towards this primary precept: one answer has to be sex, which is an essential part of having a baby. If you then apply reasoning to discover what Natural Law might rule about sexual ethics, the outcome has to be governed by whether a pregnancy can take place. That would immediately give you a ruling on the use of contraception and many others forms of sexual activity.

Let's evaluate Natural Law

STRENGTHS

- Because it can be seen as being absolutist, Natural Law provides a firm moral foundation to rules with clear guidance at all times.

- Natural Law is flexible enough to accommodate different cultures because the secondary precepts are reasoned by the society, who can interpret the primary precepts in accordance with their time and practices.

- It offers a universal moral code because most people believe in preserving life, building a good society, educating the young.

- Because this code is based on reason it is open to everyone, religious or not.

WEAKNESSES

- Some scholars have claimed that Natural Law is not totally absolutist, however Grotius argues that Natural Law holds even if there were no God because it can be reasoned along the grain of nature.

- Natural Law can be difficult to relate complex decisions to basic principles. Some philosophers have questioned this, pointing out that consequences matter in terms of human flourishing. Indeed modern philosophers like Peshcke and Gordley believe this theory is teleological and Aquinas himself seems to have agreed. When stating it was right to repay a debt, he acknowledged it would be irrational if that money was going to be used to wage war on you.

- Natural Law relies heavily on reason. This implies that human beings are capable of reasoning accurately on complex matters.

FOR DEBATE A02 skills

If a person develops a serious illness, that is part of God's plan for them. Is it therefore wrong for doctors to try and make them well again?

ACTIVITY A01 skills

In pairs prepare a presentation on Aquinas' Natural Law. You will need to show:

- its origins in Aristotle's idea of purpose
- how Aquinas developed the ideas of purpose and perfection
- why reason is an important component
- the primary and secondary precepts.

STRETCH & CHALLENGE A02 skills

Read Aquinas' response to the question about his celibacy. He said 'the precept about generation applies to the whole community, which not only must be multiplied corporeally but also make spiritual progress. And so sufficient progress is made if some only attend to generation, while others give themselves to the contemplation of divine things.'

How did he respond to the criticism? Do you find that a convincing argument in line with Natural Law?

5.5 A sense of duty

In this topic you will learn what led Kant to formulate his Ethical theory and what he understood by duty.

▮ Why is this person helping the old man across the road?

Kant (1724–1804)

It is not easy to arrive at a moral judgement when the intention and the outcome of an action appear in conflict. To clarify this, Kant sought a fixed rule that would apply to anyone in any situation; in other words an absolute moral law that was universal. To ensure it would not be clouded by emotion, he based it on the power of reason, which he believed was universal. Since judgements about outcomes are difficult unless you can predict the future accurately, Kant concentrated on a person's intention.

He believed that everybody can reason how they ought to behave in a situation, this he called 'the moral law within' (see pages 60–61). People are free to act according to this moral law or to choose to flout it. A good action undoubtedly involves following the moral law but that may not be adequate in deciding what is good and what is bad, as the situation on the left showed. When a good deed becomes tangled with a dubious intention or a bad outcome we are uncertain how good the action is.

> Good will shines forth like a precious jewel.
>
> Kant

Good will

In Kant's search for an absolute rule, there has to be no 'ifs' or 'buts' and no place for emotion. An action is only good, Kant maintained, when a person acts from a sense of good will. The action in the picture is only good if the young man has *chosen* to act out *of a sense of good will* towards another human being. In Kant's opinion, good will is the only pure motive '… it is impossible to conceive of anything at all in the world, or even out of it, which can be taken as good without qualification, *except good will'*. In his opinion all other qualities had the potential to be misused. For example, a person might act out of kindness because it made them feel good, or they wanted to appear virtuous to others. That would be a wrong action because the only valid reason is duty.

Duty for duty's sake

The only acceptable reason for putting good will into action, Kant maintained, was a sense of duty. Good will + duty = a moral action.

If you think back to most of the reasons suggested for the actions of the young man in the picture, they probably involved emotions or ulterior motives. Kant was searching for an objective definition of morality that could be applied in all situations, which meant the reasons for any action must be coldly rational and free from emotion. A person acting from a sense of duty is clearly not being forced to. Indeed Kant said 'duty involves freely choosing the action' as anything else would invalidate it. If you ask the question 'why do people do something from a sense of duty' the only answer can be 'because it is their duty to.' Any other answer would introduce a motive.

ACTIVITY

What specific duties do each of these people have?

- a dentist
- a soldier
- a checkout assistant
- a member of this class.

Are there any duties people have purely because they are members of the human race?

ACTIVITY

Think about this case that Kant discussed. A shopkeeper is always kind and friendly to you when you go into his shop. He highlights special offers and is prepared to offer you cut price deals as a regular customer. All of these will be limiting his profits. What possible reasons are there for his kind behaviour?

FOR DEBATE

There is no such thing as a sense of duty. People only act for their own ends. Looking after number one is a basic human instinct.

Ethical theories

5.6 Hypothetical and categorical imperative

In this topic you will learn what Kant means by the categorical and hypothetical imperative and his various formulations of the categorical imperative.

▊ If you want to progress round this assault course then you have to grasp that rope.

All imperatives command either hypothetically or categorically… If the action would be good simply as a means to something else, then the imperative is hypothetical; but if the action is represented as good in itself… then the imperative is categorical.

Kant

The hypothetical imperative

As you know from everyday conversation, if someone says: 'Well, let's take a hypothetical case…' then you know they are going to make up a situation to test an idea. Like the scenario in the picture, it will involve a case where if this happens, then something else follows. The reason for an action is always related to the outcome. There is no obligation to obey this imperative unless you want to achieve that outcome. For example, if you want to go on a dream holiday, then you will have to save up for it. Because Kant was searching for an absolute moral rule, what he defined as the **hypothetical imperative** was no use because these judgements were not connected with morals and they were dependent on outcome. It is useful to remember that a hypothetical imperative will begin '**If** I do this…. **then** this will happen'. This is teleological.

MAKING LINKS

A01
skills

Look back to page 60 to see how Kant also used this moral argument in his proof of the existence of God. What similarities do you notice.

The categorical imperative

For Kant the **categorical imperative** contains no uncertainty or dependence on other factors. Quite simply it says: 'You should do this.' Here Kant has a universal principle that could apply to everyone at all times. Kant broke the categorical imperative down into smaller rules, which he called **maxims**, to further define it.

CATEGORICAL IMPERATIVE

If the action is represented as good in itself ... then the imperative is categorical.

FIRST FORMULATION
Universalisation

For an action to be morally valid ... the person performing the action must not carry out any action unless he or she believes that, in the same situation, all people should act in the same way

Is it logically possible for everybody to act like this? Kant said everyone must be in a position to carry out an action. If there is any reason why that might not be possible then the action is not universal and logically invalidates it.

Do you rationally want everybody to act in this way? There cannot be one rule for one, and one for another. For a rule to be absolute, there can be no exceptions. Kant used the example of breaking a promise. Suppose you borrow money and promise to repay but know full well that you will never be able to. That action can only be right if you are prepared to let everybody else make promises they know they can't keep, which of course would make promises worthless and defies reason. He then considered laziness, which is a logical possibility for everyone. It must be wrong to be lazy, he reasoned, because we would not want it applied universally so that everybody was lazy.

SECOND FORMULATION
Humans as ends

Act that you treat humanity, both in your own person and in the person of every other human being, never merely as a means, but always at the same time as an end.

For Kant, a moral code must treat humans with respect and not just as a means to an end; humans must be the end in themselves. He regarded humanity as the highest point in God's creation, intelligent rational beings with human rights. Kant ruled out all forms of exploitation like slavery but did accept that it was possible to use people for means. So it would be acceptable to go to the doctor in order to be cured, but it would be wrong to treat people only as a means.

THIRD FORMULATION
The kingdom of ends

Act as if (you are) a legislating member in the universal kingdom of ends.

The kingdom of ends is a society made of people, all of whom are entitled to be treated as ends and not means. In this third version, Kant says everybody should act as though everyone else has the same human rights as themselves.

ACTIVITY A01 skills

Make up five statements that are hypothetical imperatives and five that are categorical imperatives.

5.5

ACTIVITY A01 skills

Design a poster to show the difference between the hypothetical and categorical imperative.

KEY WORDS

Categorical imperative: an absolute and universal sense of moral duty which directs humans to the right actions.

Maxims: rules which are derived from the categorical imperative.

ACTIVITY A01 skills

Use Kantian ethics to pass judgement on whether rape is right or wrong and give your reasoning.

FOR DEBATE A02 skills

Killing a person is always wrong. Can you universalise this?

5.7 How does Kantian ethics measure up?

In this topic you will evaluate Kantian ethics and consider the ease of applying it to situations.

▌ The person outside the car wants to know where his girlfriend is hiding. If past history is anything to go by, he is likely to harm her. The other man does know where the girl is. Should he tell the truth? What would Kant say? Why?

One of the criticisms levelled at Kantian ethics is that it relies on everyone sharing the same values and having the same sense of integrity. Some people have suggested that there is no common moral code amongst humanity: our understanding of what is right and what is wrong depends on the culture in which we have been brought up.

Although Kantian ethics went a long way towards defining an absolute moral code, many people have condemned it as cold and inhuman. Actions undertaken from a sense of love or compassion are not classed as moral by his definition, yet love and compassion are important human motivation.

For example, according to Kant the person who gives money to charity out of compassion is not doing a virtuous thing. They should only act out of duty.

'Ought' implies 'can'

Kant said that we only have a moral obligation to do our duty if we can. If circumstances prevent this, then that obligation ceases. The driver in the pictures knows he ought to tell the truth but if his mouth had been covered by sticking tape so he can't speak, then no duty exists.

ACTIVITY A02 skills

Try out Kantian ethics on this situation in order to help you decide what this moral code is like in action.

- On your way out of the door to visit your grandmother in a hospice for the terminally ill, you bump into a close friend who is really upset after a family row. What should you do?
- A blind parent asks you what you think of their new baby, which has a slight disfigurement.

ACTIVITY A01 skills

Explain why Kantian ethics are deontological.

STRETCH & CHALLENGE A01+A02 Skills

Find out how the philosopher W. D. Ross adapted Kantian ethics. Give a presentation of your findings to the group pointing out the strengths and weaknesses of this new version.

Advantages of Kantian ethics

- People generally do have the same ideas about morality.

- It is based on reason and there are clear criteria for what is moral.

- It shows respect for human life and treats everyone, even minorities, fairly.

- There is one rule for everyone which applies to all cultures and throughout time.

- Kant distinguishes between duty and inclination.

- Most people recognise the idea of duty, it is part of what it means to be human.

Disadvantages of Kantian ethics

- Putting duty above everything else seems cold and inhuman. There is no place for actions undertaken as a result of love or compassion.

- Not everyone agrees that duty is the best motive.

- Putting duty above everything else may lead to an outcome where people get hurt and you feel guilty.

- The outcome may be more important than the decision-making process.

- This abstract principle is not easy to apply in real-life situations.

- It's human nature to consider the consequences before acting.

- What happens in a situation where there is a conflict of duties? For example, how can you decide whether you should visit your gran in hospital or do your homework?

- Not everybody is capable of rational moral decision-making.

- It only works if everybody does it. If one person doesn't then everything collapses.

- Every action we take involves love and compassion because we are human creatures.

- Kantian ethics only work if everyone lives in the Kingdom of Ends.

'Is' is not the same as 'ought to'

Kant said that what is good is what we ought to do. At first sight that would appear to make sense, but think more deeply. If you apply the same notion that because something is good we ought to do it, then you will see the weakness. For example, Kant might have said, 'a dog is a good pet'. That is a **descriptive** sentence which just tells us how things are. If Kant followed his argument through he would say, 'a dog is a good pet so you ought to have a dog.' You can probably see now that there is a big difference between the 'is' part of that sentence and the 'ought' part. The second half of that sentence is **prescriptive** because it makes a rule about what we must do.

ACTIVITY

Write the FAQ section about Kant's categorical imperative for a popular website AS students consult for revision.

ACTIVITY

Select the correct terms to apply to Kantian ethics and check you are sure of the meaning: teleological or deontological; absolute or relative; synthetic or analytic; a priori or a posteriori.

FOR DEBATE

Kantian ethics won't work because people never act in a reasonable way.

ACTIVITY

Make up three statements along Kantian lines where a descriptive sentence changes to a prescriptive one and the resulting argument becomes nonsense. Now explain in your own words the problem of moving from an 'is' statement to an 'ought' statement.

KEY WORDS

A **prescriptive** statement makes a rule about how people should behave. A **descriptive** sentence simply states how things are.

5.8 What is it that everybody wants?

In this topic you will learn about Bentham's Principle of Utility and his theory of Utilitarianism.

▌ This is called the Pleasure Beach at Blackpool. What concept is behind the name of this place? How valid is that?

The search to understand the way in which we arrive at ethical judgments about behaviour led philosopher Jeremy Bentham (1748–1832) to this conclusion:

> *Nature has placed mankind under the governance of two sovereign masters, pain and pleasure. It is for them alone to point out what we ought to do, as well as to determine what we shall do.*

You will notice that Bentham has removed goodness as being something inherent in an action. What he is looking at is the outcome of an action.

Bentham is described as a hedonist, which means someone who dedicates their life to the search for pleasure. The Hedonists were a group of ancient Greeks who sought true pleasure which has no pain in it. Twenty-first century society is frequently described as hedonistic but this is different because alcohol and consumerism often have painful consequences.

Pleasure or pain?

Bentham said that when anyone has to decide on a right or wrong course of action, they ask themselves: 'What is the most useful thing to do in this situation?' What they are actually weighing up is which path will lead them to the greatest pleasure. He called this the **Principle of Utility**:

By the principle of utility is meant that property of any object, whereby it tends to produce benefit, advantage, pleasure, good, or happiness (all this in the present case comes to the same thing) or (what comes again to the same thing) to prevent the happening of mischief, pain, evil, or unhappiness to the party whose interest is considered: if that party be the community in general, the happiness of the community: if a particular individual, then the happiness of that individual.

Can you measure pleasure?

Bentham thought you could. He lived in a time of major scientific advances, and in his opinion pleasure was not something abstract, but measurable. He devised a chart to quantify the pain or pleasure caused by an action. It is called the **Hedonic Calculus**.

- Intensity of pleasure.
- Duration of pleasure.
- How certain is it that pleasure will result?
- How near is the pleasure to you?
- How continuous is the pleasure?
- Is there likely to be pain mixed with this pleasure?
- How widespread will the pleasure be?

ACTIVITY A02 skills

Choose two different activities (e.g. having a tattoo, studying for A levels) and apply Bentham's Hedonic Calculus to them. How useful is it as a measure? Is that the outcome you agree with? Try working through some common examples in the group then compare results to find out whether the responses are common or individual.

STRETCH & CHALLENGE A02 skills

'It is vain to talk of the interest of the community, without understanding what is the interest of the individual'. How could Bentham use Utilitarian ethics to create laws?

The strengths of Bentham's Utilitarianism

- It provides a clear, mathematical method of deciding any course of action by balancing pleasure and pain which makes it easy to compare different options.

- It is a popular approach to ethics because people do seek pleasure and avoid pain.

- It looks at the consequences of an action.

- Common sense is involved, this ethical code is accessible to everyone.

Can you spot its weaknesses?

5.9 Mill develops the Utilitarian argument

In this topic you will examine and assess the way John Stuart Mill developed Bentham's theory.

▌ 'It is better to be a human being satisfied than a pig satisfied; better to be Socrates dissatisfied than a fool satisfied.' What point is Mill making and what is the connection with Bentham's argument?

ACTIVITY **A02** skills

Consider the difference between what might give a pig, a fool and Socrates pleasure. Would you say any of those pleasures are of a superior quality, or is it simply a matter of taste?

Because John Stuart Mill's father, James, had been a follower of Bentham, the son grew up well steeped in Utilitarian philosophy. Mill regarded Bentham as 'the father of English innovation, both in doctrines and in institutions.' Mill's knowledge put him in an excellent position to appraise and revise the eighteenth-century philosopher's thinking.

ACTIVITY **A01** skills

List six pleasures you think Mill would rank as higher pleasures and six he would rank as lower pleasures.

Weaknesses in Bentham's Utilitarian argument

- The emphasis on pleasure Mill saw as little more than animal instincts: e.g. the pursuit of sex, food and drink.

- Bentham does not distinguish between different sorts of pleasures or give them any rank order.

- What is pleasure for one person may not be for another, and may indeed cause pain.

- The Hedonic Calculus is not easy to apply and certainly not practical when faced with a situation requiring a quick response.

ACTIVITY **A02** skills

Re-enact a confrontation between Jeremy Bentham and John Stuart Mill who are guests on the TV show 'Wine, Women and Song'.

- Bentham's Utilitarianism relies on accurately predicting the consequences of an action. That is not always possible.

- Decisions favour 'the greatest number' of people, which means the wishes of minority groups are ignored.

- Some people make decisions that are not designed to bring them personal pleasure.

Quantity isn't everything

The pigs on the opposite page demonstrate Mill's rejection of the Hedonic Calculus, which measures the *quantity* of pleasure involved and equates one form of pleasure with another. That was not an oversight on Bentham's part. He had stated: 'All things being equal, pushpin [a game] is equal to poetry.' Mill did not agree. In his view some pleasures are of a higher *quality* than others because they engage those parts of the brain which distinguish humans from animals in intelligence. **Higher pleasures** satisfy the mind, **lower pleasures** please the body.

Mill was a great admirer of Bentham and whilst he might disagree with parts of his philosophy, he believed in the Principle of Utility. Bentham had said it was not possible to prove this principle but Mill showed it was. He argued that:

- Happiness is a desirable state of affairs.

- Happiness is the *only* desirable thing. Other things only seem desirable because they lead to happiness.

- The general happiness of all is desirable because if everyone is happy, your happiness increases.

Rule Utilitarianism

Through his philosophy, Mill tried to define Utilitarianism in a way that made it practical to use when creating rules for society. Unlike Bentham, Mill concentrated on how decisions are reached so the greatest good is given to the greatest number of people in a society. This could of course mean that individual pleasure is sacrificed to the community. Nobody gets pleasure from paying a bus fare, but the community gets pleasure from a good public transport system. Mill believed a society had to have general rules arrived at by Utilitarian reasoning, in order to operate. These needed to be generally agreed and accepted for a society to operate. His example was that it is necessary to tell the truth because that leads to the greatest happiness of the greatest number.

Act Utilitarianism

Bentham's brand of Utilitarianism judged every situation individually and in isolation from the community. In every case he asked what action would bring about the greatest good. This means every action is judged on its own merits and individual circumstances taken into consideration, which gives it the merit of being flexible but is time-consuming to operate. Critics say this could be used to justify almost anything.

Ethical theories

5.10 How useful is Utilitarianism in the modern world?

In this topic you will evaluate Utilitarianism as an ethical code and consider recent developments in this argument.

ACTIVITY   A01 skills

Paraphrase these two extracts where Mill is considering the voice of the minority.

If mankind minus one were of one opinion, then mankind is no more justified in silencing the one than the one – if he had the power – would be justified in silencing mankind.

The only freedom which deserves the name is that of pursuing our own good, in our own way, so long as we do not attempt to deprive others of theirs, or impeded their efforts to obtain it.

▋ How would a Utilitarian explain to a worker in this sweat shop the morality of paying them low wages to make cheap garments for the western world?

Utilitarianism, like other ethical theories, is offered as a way of making a moral judgement about the right and wrong way of behaviour. Let's consider how useful it is for arriving at personal decisions and communal decisions.

Mill was concerned that Bentham's Utilitarianism favoured the wishes of the majority at the expense of the minority. It was a philosophy that could justify slavery, modern exploitation such as that in the picture above, and even torture if the number of sadists enjoying it outweighed the number of victims.

ACTIVITY A02 skills

What do you think constitutes happiness? How would you measure it? Is it an acceptable basis for an ethical code?

Strong Utilitarianism and Weak Utilitarianism

Bentham's Utilitarianism offered a straightforward approach to arriving at moral decisions with one simple rule, the Principle of Utility. It is referred to as 'Strong Utilitarianism' because Bentham insisted the principle must be adhered to without exceptions.

Mill's 'Weak Utilitarianism' took a more flexible approach, accepting there might be occasions when it was necessary to break the principle if the consequences of the action were harmful. The example of truth-telling he gave (see page 113) was qualified with the understanding that telling the truth could be set aside if it would result in harm. You might like to reconsider the situation in the picture on page 108.

Preference Utilitarianism

Preference Utilitarianism developed in the twentieth century with philosophers such as R.M. Hare (1919–2002) and, more recently, Peter Singer (born in 1946) sought a way of decision-making that would take account of the views of minorities. Preference Utilitarians consider whether a decision is right or wrong by asking whether it fits in with what people would rationally prefer.

Singer was as concerned as Mill about the rights of minorities: '*Our preferences cannot count any more than the preferences of others*,' Singer wrote. He went on to say that everyone's individual preferences must be taken into consideration when deciding what was in the best interests of the group. By doing that, he believed everyone's interests were given equal value.

He also went on to argue that the right thing to do is what is in *the best interests* of the greatest number, rather than simply the result of calculating pleasure against pain.

What Singer's approach to Utilitarianism does is concentrate on minimising suffering, rather than maximising pleasure. He believes there is a far greater agreement about what causes pain that what gives pleasure. You might like to consider whether pleasure is more down to personal preference than pain is.

Advantages of Utilitarian ethics

- It is a simple and common sense philosophy which people in the twenty-first century feel able to apply.

- It is fair and suits a democratic society.

- Considering the consequences of an action comes naturally to people.

- It is a universal rule, applicable whatever the culture, religion or society.

Disadvantages of Utilitarian ethics

- You have to know what gives other people happiness, or what is in their best interests. How can you be sure? What if one person's idea of happiness involves giving pain to another?

- No account is taken of situations where a person wants to do something irrespective of the consequences.

- It relies on accurate predictions of the outcome.

- A rule that benefits those involved is not always applicable in all situations.

- No account is taken of situations where the wrong motives lead to the right outcome.

STRETCH & CHALLENGE

Research Henry Sidgwick's contribution to Utilitarianism. Sidgwick (1838–1900) is widely regarded as the third big name associated with this philosophy. You might also like to investigate the contribution of R. M. Hare, a leading twentieth-century Utilitarian philosopher and an influence on Peter Singer. Produce a diagram to show how your chosen philosopher took Bentham and Mill's concepts forward.

FOR DEBATE

Do you agree that attempting to maximise people's preferences takes into account minority views?

ACTIVITY

Try out the different forms of Utilitarian decision-making processes on the situations below and assess how they work.

- You arrange to go and visit your elderly granny who is unconscious and dying in hospital only to discover a childhood friend is having a leaving party.
- Your younger sister is trapped in the burning house. Do you risk your life and perhaps those of the fire service by going in to get her or leave her to die?

5.11 How Christian ethics relates to other ethical theories

In this topic you will make links between Christian ethics and the other ethical theories featured in this chapter.

NATURAL LAW

GOD

BIBLE

ORDERLY

WORLD

BAD

GOOD

KANTIAN ETHICS

MORAL LAW WITHIN

Emotion

DUTY = VIRTUE + HAPPINESS

THE ULTIMATE END

SUMMUM BONUM

5.12 What is the relationship between morality and Christianity?

In this topic you will examine the connection between ethical theories and Christianity and consider whether morality can exist apart from religion.

What is the connection between morality and religion?

It is obvious that there is a very strong link between morality and religion because you are studying ethics as part of Religious Studies, yet some of the ethical theories you have studied would be acceptable to an atheist. As ethics deals with decisions about what is right and wrong in life, there is a clear overlap with religion. Equally, ethical theories arise out of their time and culture and may well be influenced by religion. Religion is concerned with all aspects of God's creation, both the natural world and humanity, and formulates rules for their inter-relationship. For this exam you can study the religious ethics of any religion. In this textbook we have chosen to examine Christian ethics.

■ One of the traditional concepts of God is as law-giver and judge of every person's behaviour. This, of course, gives God a very central place in moral decision-making.

ACTIVITY

Take a moral issue such as stealing and construct an ideas map showing all the possible sources of information that could shape your decision that stealing is wrong.

Autonomy: Morality existing independently of religion. Its ideas are shaped by reason alone.

Heteronomy: Morality shaped by religious belief. Its rules are taken directly from religious teachings.

RELATIONSHIP BETWEEN RELIGION AND ETHICS

Theonomy: The principles and values behind both religious and ethical rules are the same.

The Euthyphro dilemma

The connection between religion and ethics has long fascinated philosophers and goes back at least to Plato. In one of his works called *Euthyphro*, the character of Socrates asks: 'Is something right because the gods command it or do the gods command it because it is right?'

Euthyphro's dilemma for Christians

On the one hand the argument is saying that whatever God commands is good in itself, and we cannot apply reason or verify it in anyway. If God were to command a cruel or dishonest action, then it would be right simply because he commanded it.

The other argument is saying that there are a set of absolute rules which are separate from God but known to him. God has not made these rules right, he merely commanded humans to follow them.

The Divine Command theory

This argument is that something is good simply because God commands it and for no other reason. Here you might recognise one side of Euthyphro's argument.

Many Christian thinkers, including Aquinas and Luther, and more recently William Temple and Pope John Paul II, have rejected the Divine Command theory because they say some things are innately good or bad. Temple said, 'In its nature, the moral judgment is quite wholly independent of religion.'

Can morality exist separately from religion?

The Humanists, a group of people who reject religion, believe it can. Read what A. J. Ayer said:

> Humanism is an approach to life based on reason and our common humanity, recognising that moral values are properly founded on human nature and experience alone. Humanists value ideas for which there is evidence, and the things inside and around us that make life worth living.
>
> Humanists believe that moral values are not dependent on religion and that it is untrue, unfair to non-religious people and a damaging idea in an increasingly secular society to assert otherwise. Humanists believe that moral values evolved, and continue to evolve, along with human nature and society and are indeed based on human nature, experience and society. If human civilisation were to develop all over again, it is highly unlikely that exactly the same religions would develop. But it is very likely that our basic moral principles would be the same, because human beings, who have evolved to live in groups, need the kinds of rules which enable us to live together co-operatively and harmoniously …

FOR DEBATE A01 skills

What is the difference in meaning between the two parts of the Euthyphro dilemma? Which part of Euthyphro's dilemma would give God supreme power? How?

ACTIVITY A02 skills

In pairs try arguing the two sides of Euthyphro's dilemma with one of you taking the role of the Christian who believes God is good and the other trying to find weaknesses in that argument.

ACTIVITY A02 skills

Write a justification of A.J. Ayers' statement.

ACTIVITY A01 skills

Write a paragraph explaining how morality and religion could be seen as separate issues.

5.13 What do Christians use to make ethical decisions?

In this topic you will study the different sources of Christian ethics and consider the implications of basing a moral code on each source.

Christians set out to follow the Will of God. They use various different sources of authority to discover what the Will of God is and the diagram below gives some ideas of the main ones. Whilst most Christians would recognise these as sources of authority, they are likely to place a different emphasis on their relative importance. Although the diagram shows them as separate entities, you will notice that many overlap or are linked by similar ideas.

Bible

Christians believe the scriptures transmit the Word of God: this gives them authority. The weight of authority given to the Bible is dependent on what exactly a Christian believes about these books.

Some Christians believe that humans were inspired by God to write down the scriptures which means the writings are related to the time and culture when they were recorded and may contain human errors. This makes them a useful source of guidance to people but does not make their contents absolute.

Others believe the Bible contains God's words handed down directly to humans. This makes these writings divine and makes them the highest authority – their rules and ethical codes are absolute.

The New Testament has particular importance for Christians because it records the teachings of Jesus, whom Christians regard as God's Son sent to earth to save humanity. They also believe it is essential to follow Jesus' teachings if they are to be saved.

CHRISTIAN AUTHORITY

Church

The authority of the Church comes from several sources. Christian priests have a vocation and training that enables them to interpret and transmit the Word of God and the teachings of Jesus to others. Church tradition, which is based on the interpretation of the Bible, is important in Christian ethical decision-making.

In the book of Acts, there is an account of the early Church being inspired directly by the Holy Spirit which Christians believe continues to inspire it today. This gives the Church authority to formulate ethical codes for Christians, based on the scriptures.

STRETCH & CHALLENGE

A01 skills

Research Aristotle's theory of Virtue Ethics, which says that moral actions determine the nature of our character. How did Aquinas develop this? What does Virtue Ethics add to Christian ethics?

The Holy Spirit

Christians believe that after Jesus ascended, God continued to reveal himself to humanity through the Holy Spirit. Individuals through prayer, groups of Christians through worship or the Church as a whole, may receive revelations from the Holy Spirit which help them formulate an ethical code. Revelation gives an ethical code great authority.

Conscience

Christians regard their conscience as the ultimate guide for making moral decisions because it was given to them by God and represents the voice of the Holy Spirit within them. Prayer, worship and the teachings of the Church also assist the conscience, which Aquinas described as reason-making moral decisions.

Love

For some Christians the source of authority for moral decision-making is simply love. They base their argument on the idea that God is love and Jesus' words and actions showed that love was the primary factor in any situation. Gospel stories show Jesus was prepared to set aside the authority of Jewish law if necessary when deciding on the most loving action in a situation.

Reason and Natural Law

Christians believe there is a Natural Law, which is God-given and as such has authority in the formulation of an ethical code. Humans have been given the power of reasoning by God in order to understand this Natural Law which provides a reliable guide to what is good and what is evil.

ACTIVITY

A02 skills

Examine each source to determine which might be absolutist and which relativist. To do this, consider which source puts the onus on the individual to discover the morality of an action and which provides outside guidance.

121

Ethical theories

5.14 What are the main ethical principles of Christianity?

In this topic you will examine the main ethical principles of Christianity and consider how Christians use them to reach decisions.

❚ Some people believe that God handed the Ten Commandments directly to humanity. This gives that moral code huge significance and makes the rules absolute.

ACTIVITY A01 skills

Analyse the Sermon on the Mount (Matthew 5:3–11). How is Jesus telling people to behave? What appears to underpin these ethical teachings?

ACTIVITY A01 skills

Analyse the accounts in Matthew 15:1–9; Luke 13:10–16. Outline the situation. What action did the Jewish ethical code demand? What did Jesus do? What was he basing his actions on?

ACTIVITY A01 skills

Read Matthew 5. How does Jesus see his role in relation to the Jewish ethical code?

A Jewish foundation

Christianity has its roots in Judaism because Jesus was born and brought up as a Jew. His moral code came from that religious tradition and this is reflected in the Christian scriptures because the largest section of the Bible is the Old Testament also known as the Hebrew Bible. Many Jews believe the first five books of the Bible contain the precise words God gave humanity in order that they could lead good lives. Jewish teachers over the centuries have applied reason to interpret these rules so they can be applied to daily life. The moral principle behind Jewish ethics is that God is just and loving. This was summed up by the prophet Micah (Micah 6:8) who wrote: 'The Lord has told us what is good. What he requires of us is this: to do what is just, to show constant love, and to live in humble fellowship with our God.'

For Christians the Old Testament contains important ethical rules, the most important being the Ten Commandments. For some Christians and Jews these are a set of deontological and absolute rules.

The ethics of Jesus

Because Christians believe Jesus was the Son of God, everything he did or said on earth is given the same status as though it came directly from God. If any of his teachings conflict with ethical codes in the Old Testament, Jesus' words take precedence.

The New Testament contains many examples where Jesus acted out of love or compassion and deliberately set aside Jewish rules. When challenged by a Jewish scholar about the most important of the rules, Jesus replied: '"Love the Lord your God with all your heart, with all your soul, and with all your mind." This is the greatest and the most important commandment. The second is: "Love your neighbour as you love yourself." The whole Law of Moses and the teachings of the prophets depend on these two commandments.' (Matthew 22: 37–40). This is often referred to as the Golden Rule.

The emphasis on putting love into action is at the heart of Christianity. Jesus developed his teachings on this in the Sermon on the Mount, which appears in Matthew 5:3–11.

Following Jesus' teachings is what God wants and this will lead believers to the Kingdom of Heaven and ultimate union with God.

The role of St Paul in Christian ethics

Jesus' teachings were interpreted in the years following Jesus' death by the apostle Paul. Paul's interpretation of Jesus' ethics have had the most profound influence on the development of Christianity. Paul maintained that followers of Jesus did not need a legalistic code because 'their conduct shows that what the Law commands is written in their hearts. Their consciences also show that this is true, since their thoughts sometimes accuse them and sometimes defend them' (Romans 2:14–15).

Paul also developed Jesus' emphasis on the law of love as the main ethical rule. All other ethical decisions arise naturally from this. The love Paul refers to is agape and his famous letter to the people of Corinth (I Corinthians 13) explains exactly how Paul sees love in action. Paul's insistence of love being the principal factor in an ethical decision is developed from Jesus' teaching that people should love God first and then their fellow men.

MAKING LINKS *A01 skills*

Can you identify where St Paul is using Natural Law in his argument?

ACTIVITY *A01 skills*

Define *agape* and explain how it differs from other forms of love.

STRETCH & CHALLENGE *A01+A02 skills*

What is the Christian theologian Reinhold Niebuhr's objection to using love as the basis of ethical decision making?

'I still believe, as I believed then, that love may be the motive of social action but that justice must be the instrument of love in the world in which self-interest is bound to defy the canons of love at every level.' Do you agree?

ACTIVITY *A01 skills*

Create a poster or diagram that explains clearly how Christian ethics evolved from Jewish foundations, through the teachings of Jesus and subsequently of St Paul. This will make an excellent revision aid, so be sure to display the key areas that were taken forward and developed as well as those that became dead ends.

Ethical theories

5.15 How does Christian ethics measure up as an ethical theory?

In this topic you will consider Christian ethics alongside the other ethical theories we have studied and evaluate it.

▌ Roman Catholic Christians use this book for guidance on the Church's teachings and traditions on a large number of areas of life. Is that a deontological or teleological approach to ethics?

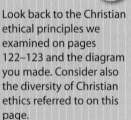
Are Christian ethics absolute or relativist?

Because Christianity is such a large world religion, it is not surprising that there is a wide spectrum of interpretations within it. The diagram on pages 120–121 showed some of the major sources of authority Christians use when arriving at an ethical decision. Roman Catholic Christianity places great emphasis on the traditions of the Church in interpreting the scriptures. This means the Catholic Church, led by the Pope, is the principal source of authority and Aquinas' Natural Law is the main ethical theory that underpins it. You will recall from earlier work (see pages 98–99) that Aquinas argued that some things are right in themselves and others wrong.

Within Protestant Christianity there is also a wide interpretation of Christian ethics with some evangelical Christians taking an absolute approach to Biblical codes of behaviour. This applies not only to ethical codes such as the Ten Commandments but also to other Old Testament laws against homosexuality and abortion. More liberal Protestants base their ethical code around Jesus' command to show unconditional love to God first and then to others. This would be their absolute rule, but the application of this rule could be considered relativist.

One controversial Protestant ethical theory is Situation Ethics. Arising from Jesus' approach to love as the single most important factor in a moral decision, Joseph Fletcher developed his theory in the 1960s. He argued that when faced with a moral dilemma, the right course of action is the most loving thing to do. The action might go against Biblical teachings and indeed might go against the laws of the country, but according to Fletcher it is the correct Christian ethic. This ethical theory considers every situation separately and applies reason to it.

How does Christianity compare to other ethical codes that we have studied?

Utilitarianism

On the face of it this ethical theory would seem to have a great deal in common with Christian ethics. The philosopher Paley certainly thought so. He wrote that virtue is 'doing good to mankind, in obedience to the will of God, and for the sake of everlasting happiness.' Despite being atheist himself, Bentham was sure Christians would support the Utilitarian argument because they regard God as good and John Stuart Mill likened the principle of Utility to Jesus' Golden Rule. Utilitarianism and Christianity do have different targets. According to Jesus, his followers must put other people's needs ahead of their own, which is not a Utilitarian principle. Christianity does also have some deontological rules such as the Ten Commandments whereas Utilitarianism is teleological. A key objection to Utilitarianism is its lack of rights.

Kantian ethics

This ethical code also appears to have much in common with Christianity because it places great emphasis on treating people as an end in themselves. Kant's universality also seems to have echoes in Jesus' Golden Rule but Kant's universality requires rigid rules and actions determined by reason alone. This is not the way most Christians make ethical judgments.

Natural Law

You have probably noticed that the philosophers involved in the creation of this philosophy were Christians and so the two philosophies are extremely close. Indeed Natural Law forms the basis of Roman Catholic ethics. Protestant ethics shares only parts of this philosophy and in areas such as Situation Ethics can deviate a great deal.

STRETCH & CHALLENGE *A01 skills*

Investigate further Joseph Fletcher's Theory of Situation Ethics. Decide what philosophical labels can be assigned to it, in terms of deontological, teleological, a priori, a posteriori, etc. What are its strengths and weaknesses as a moral code?

STRETCH & CHALLENGE *A01+A02 Skills*

The Gospels said that Jesus was not breaking the Jewish law but fulfilling and completing it. What does that mean for Christian ethics?

It is worth remembering that for Christians, faith in God and Jesus is the most important requirement. This is not a religion that places great emphasis on obeying religious rules. What is considered more important is to act in the same way as Jesus did. How would you define that sort of ethics?

ExamCafé

Relax, refresh, result!

Relax and prepare

Absolute and relative ethics

Junaid

We did this topic first and it did not make much sense until we revised it at the end of the course. I really wish we just learnt what the words meant and then applied them to each theory as we went through.

Akshar

I think that this is correct. Absolute ethics are laws which are right or wrong for all people for all time, whereas relative ethics change depending on the time, place, culture and situation involved. Kantian ethics and Natural Law are absolute and Utilitarianism is relative.

Zane

We had to research what the words 'absolute' and 'relative' mean as a homework task so we really learnt what they meant for ourselves. We also developed our own examples to back each one up so that we could use them again and again. For example: teleological ethics are ethics which look at the end result, so if giving to charity means lives can be saved then giving to charity is a good action.

Dena

My teacher gave each member of the class one of these words as a 'pet' and we won prizes every time we managed to link what we were doing in class with our 'pet' topic. This worked really well but I know relativism much better than absolutism because that was my 'pet'.

Refresh your memory

Revision checklist for absolute and relative ethics

In order to do well in this topic you will need to:

▷ Understand the concepts of absolute and relativist morality.

▷ Understand what it means to call an ethical theory absolutist and objective.

▷ Understand what it means to call an ethical theory relativist and subjective.

▷ Understand the terms deontological and teleological.

Common Mistakes

▷ The most common mistake students make is to confuse absolute and relative morality. It is easy to see that a student knows the difference but has got the words mixed up; what is harder is to award the marks the student deserves.

▷ To avoid making this mistake always try to link any theory you study to these ideas.

Keep asking yourself: is this theory absolute or relative? Is it subjective or objective? Is it deontological or teleological? It is always a good idea to have a list written down showing which theories are absolute and which are relative. For example, Kantian ethics are absolute and Utilitarianism is relative.

Get the result!

Examiner's tips

If candidates were asked to outline the strengths or weakness of either absolutist or relativist ethics, or deontological or teleological ethics, what I might expect is an answer which includes the following ideas:

● A clear definition of absolute/ relative or deontological/ teleological ethics.

● Using specific examples: for example, 'Natural law is an example of an absolutist ethic.'

● Outlining the strengths and/or weaknesses in clear paragraphs with evidence to support each point.

● Where appropriate, linking the ideas to specific situations. For example, 'Utilitarianism is good for euthanasia because …'

Read the essay below about absolute and relative ethics and decide for yourself what makes it a good answer:

Rachel's answer

Absolute ethics have one main weakness: this is that they will never change or adapt to a situation . Absolute ethical theories are for all people for all time and will not change depending on cultural differences. Although this gives people clear rules to follow in all situations it does not allow for different circumstances. The Ten Commandments are a good example of absolute ethics. This is because they are fixed in stone, literally. They are good for applying to abortion and euthanasia as they say that people should not be killed. Kantian ethics are also absolute because they are based on a fixed moral maxim which is universalised. Therefore if killing is wrong then even if you have to kill one person to save the lives of a million others, an absolute ethical theory would still say that it is wrong.

However, relative morality is linked to things like culture, time, place or the situations and will change when the time, place culture or situation changes. For example if you use Utilitarianism in a very general way you will vary your ethical actions based on what will bring about the greatest happiness to the greatest number of people. So if an abortion will stop a severely disabled foetus having a really poor quality of life and save the mother from a more difficult life this may bring the greatest happiness to the greatest numbers. This can also work against relativism. If having an abortion will mean that a mother and her partner can enjoy a three week skiing holiday later in the year and not have to spend money on a child then Utilitarianism would also agree with its outcome.

Therefore, relative ethics are of more use than absolute ethics because they can adapt to situations, but they can be misused.

ExamCafé
Relax, refresh, result!

Relax and prepare

Hot tips

Natural Law

Phil

What I found really difficult was getting my head around that word 'natural'. In my first essay I wrote that everything was natural and if it was natural then it was right. My teacher corrected me, saying that Aquinas observed human nature and used his reason to determine what we should do. The example that I will always remember (if only because I disagree with it so much!) is that the purpose of our reproductive organs is to reproduce, so homosexual sex is seen as wrong by Natural Law because it goes against the purpose of those organs, against the primary precept of continuation of the species.

Akshar

I really liked Natural Law; it is very logical and it gives clear rules. However, it also gives you the chance to think for yourself when reasoning the secondary precepts. This is better than strict rules like the Ten Commandments.

Aisha

I prefer Utilitarianism to Natural Law because Utilitarianism is relative, unlike Natural Law. I like this because you cannot apply one rule to every situation because not every situation is the same. Also, it is easy to work out what makes people happy but using reason could lead to any conclusion.

Refresh your memory

Revision checklist for Natural Law

In order to do well in this topic you will need to:

▷ Understand the origins of St Thomas Aquinas' Natural Law in Aristotle's idea of purpose.

▷ Understand Aquinas' ideas of purpose and perfection.

▷ Understand the use of reason to discover Natural Law.

▷ Understand the primary and secondary precepts.

▷ Explain real and apparent goods.

▷ Explain interior and exterior acts.

▷ Understand and explain criticisms of Natural Law.

▷ Analyse and compare the views and assess their strengths and weaknesses.

Get the result!

How to plan your answer

Any part a) Natural Law exam question will expect candidates to explain the basic principles of Natural Law. But a really good way to start is to explain about purpose and the fact that everything seems to be striving to fulfil its purpose. This way you can bring in Aquinas' link to Aristotle.

Then you could go on to talk about specific aspects of the Natural Law theory such as:

- 'do good and avoid evil'
- the primary precepts and the use of reason to establish the secondary precepts
- the difference between real and apparent goods and interior and exterior acts.

Remember, you must be specific and use the correct terms. This will get you higher marks. For example, if you use terminology, make sure that you use it correctly and spell it correctly. If you use examples, don't just focus on an example you can remember straightaway that sort of fits: try to use really specific examples to back up each point you make.

Quite often questions will also ask you to apply Natural Law to ethical dilemmas or other ethical theories. You will need to show how each element of Natural Law may relate to an issue /dilemma or ethical theory. For example, what similarities and differences are there between the primary precepts and sanctity of life or the secondary precepts and the Hedonic Calculus?

Practice questions

To prepare for the exam you need to make sure you know the key terms involved and, most importantly, that you can explain them with examples. Answer the following questions and use your responses to target your revision.

1. What does purpose mean?
2. How would the primary precepts relate to abortion?
3. Invent a secondary precept to deal with euthanasia.
4. How might real and apparent goods relate to war?
5. What is wrong with Aristotle's idea of purpose?
6. Write five criticisms of the primary and secondary precepts.
7. Compare Natural Law to Utilitarianism: what is similar about them? What is different?
8. Which is a better ethical theory: Natural Law or Kant's ethical theory?
9. Does the religious aspect make Natural Law stronger or weaker? Why?

Now look at the extract from an essay on the right and make a list of its strengths and weaknesses.

St Thomas Aquinas used his understanding of Aristotle to help develop his ideas of Natural Law. Aquinas believed we have a purpose to do good and avoid evil, thus at the end of our lives we will unite with God. He believed we know which actions are right and which are wrong through the use of our reason, however sometimes bad logic could lead to the wrong moral choices. Aquinas developed the primary precepts which follow from the idea of doing good and avoiding evil. The primary precepts are concerned with self preservation and the preservation of the innocent, the education of children, the continuation of the species through reproduction, worshipping God and living in society. From these Aquinas develops secondary precepts. For example, from the primary precept of self preservation and the preservation of the innocent one could argue that life saving medical care such as a blood transfusion would be acceptable. This could lead to a secondary precept of give blood to save the lives of yourself and others.

ExamCafé
Relax, refresh, result!

Relax and prepare

Kantian ethics

Mark

Read Kant carefully and make sure you understand his ideas before you try to answer a question on his ethical theory. Kant can be a bit tricky the first time around!

Dean

When you write about the three formulations of the categorical imperative you need to include examples with them. It is best to make up your own examples. When I did this for myself I found that I understood the topic much better and I could always remember these examples and use them in my essays.

Claire

I always got the hypothetical and categorical imperatives mixed up. I always had to refer to my notes to remember which is which. My friend ended up telling me that cats were better than hippos!! It meant that the *cat*egorical imperatives are better than the *hypo*thetical imperatives. A bit silly – but it worked!

Emma

There are lots of new words to learn with Kant, so I made myself a glossary. This really helped me remember what everything meant.

Refresh your memory

Revision checklist for Kantian ethics

In order to do well in this topic you will need to:

▷ Understand and explain Kant's theory of duty – (duty for duty's sake).
▷ Understand and explain the moral law (known through reason).
▷ Understand and explain good will (can be linked to Christian idea of 'treat others as you wish to be treated').
▷ Understand and explain summum bonum (the ultimate end).
▷ Understand hypothetical imperative (if I do x I will get y).

▷ Understand categorical imperative (I ought to do).
▷ Compare hypothetical imperative and categorical imperative.
▷ Understand and explain the universalisation of maxims. (Test against the contradiction of will and contradiction against nature.)
▷ Understand the three formulations of the categorical imperative (universalisation, ends not means to an end, Kingdom of Ends).
▷ Evaluate Kantian ethics.

Get the result!

Sample answers

Exam question

(a) Explain Kant's theory of duty with reference to the hypothetical and categorical imperatives.
(25 marks)

Examiner says

Many students make the mistake of writing everything they know about a topic rather than actually answering the question set. Oz has answered a question about the categorical imperative and you can see that he sets it in context without writing everything he knows, then explains the categorical imperative in some detail with some good examples. The examples help Oz to show that he really does understand Kant's ideas. Without the examples it would be harder to award the higher marks.

Oz's answer

Kant believed that people should always do their duty, because it is their duty to do so. He believed that they should not do it for themselves but because it is the good thing to do in following your duty. He said that there are two types of imperative: categorical imperative and hypothetical imperative. Categorical imperatives are things which you must do, whereas, hypothetical imperatives are conditional and depend on the person and circumstances, for example if you want to lose weight you should not eat doughnuts.

Kant said that the categorical imperatives are the only moral choice and hypothetical imperative is wrong and shouldn't be followed as they will result in pleasure for the person following them alone. There are three principles or formulations involved in the categorical imperative;

1. The universal law: this means making sure that you set a maxim which can be universalised so that it can apply to anyone, anywhere, for all time without any contradiction. For example, 'do not lie' is a maxim which can be universalised without contradiction.

2. Treat people as ends in themselves: this means not using them to achieve something else or a means to an end. This ensures equality, as all humans have equal value and should not be enslaved or exploited.

3. Acting as though you live in a kingdom of ends; this is a combination of the first two principles and state that if everyone does their duty and acts in a just and civilised manner, then society will become just and civilised. Kant believed that we should be law makers in the kingdom of ends.

Examiner tips

I would like candidates to explain that Kant's theory of duty is deontological and focuses on the idea of a moral law. I hope they explain Kant's understanding of good will and duty and the link between them. It would be good if candidates explained that Kant saw moral statements as categorical and explain the categorical imperative and its various formulations. For me a good response would contrast the categorical and hypothetical imperatives. But an even better answer would refer to Kant's examples and explain how Kant rejected consequentialism.

Some exam questions will expect you to evaluate Kant's ideas. This is a test of your understanding of Kant's ideas and the ability to be able to discuss these strengths and weaknesses in relations to an ethical issue. For example, you may need to say if Kant is a good approach to a topic such as human embryo research. So you will need to explain Kant's strengths and weaknesses and use a topic such as human embryo research to help illustrate and evaluate these strengths and weaknesses.

ExamCafé

Relax, refresh, result!

Hot tips

Utilitarianism

Dave

GGFTGN is a useful way to remember the **g**reatest **g**ood **f**or **t**he **g**reatest **n**umber. My teacher always teaches us silly rhymes to help us remember the different areas of Utilitarianism.

Phee

When I think of Utilitarianism all I can ever remember is GGFTGN (Greatest good for the greatest number), but I always get Bentham and Mill, act and rule mixed up. I can't remember what's in the Hedonic Calculus and Singer's ideas didn't even register even though I've got loads of notes on it!

Michaela

I remember the Hedonic Calculus using **PREDICT**. I remember that the Hedonic Calculus has to **predict** the amount of happiness will bring and the seven factors of the Hedonic Calculus are: **P**urity, **R**emoteness, **E**xtent, **D**uration, **I**ntensity, **C**ertainty, **T**o be followed by…

Examiner's tips

Examiners see a lot of candidates like Phee every year. They have the right information but they mix up the names. To get good marks candidates really must use the terminology accurately.

Refresh your memory

Revision checklist for Utilitarianism

In order to do well in this topic you will need to:

▷ Understand and explain the principle of utility (usefulness, greatest amount of happiness).

▷ Understand Bentham's utility – Greatest Good For The Greatest Number.

▷ Understand Mill's Utilitarianism – (quality not quantity).

▷ Compare Bentham and Mill's Utilitarianism.

▷ Explain Hedonism (two sovereign meters = pleasure and pain).

▷ Explain Hedonic Calculus (know and can apply the seven factors).

▷ Mill's criticisms of Bentham and his ideas of qualitative not quantitative pleasures.

▷ Explain higher and lower pleasures (mind versus body).

▷ Understand and explain Act and Rule Utilitarianism (actions leading to greatest versus general rules for the good of the community).

▷ Singer's Preference Utilitarianism (best interests of those affected).

▷ Evaluate Utilitarianism (strengths and weaknesses).

Get the result!

Examiner says

This is a good answer because Sarah has given a clear and concise outline of Bentham and Mill's ideas. She has used the correct terminology and shown how and why Mill changed Bentham's ideas. Sarah has also given a good example to support and help her explanation of Mill's ideas. What would make it even better would be if Sarah included some more examples to support her explanation. For example, she could have explained in more detail each element of the Hedonic Calculus and given a specific example for each one. This would have helped show the examiner that she really understood the topic and attracted good marks.

Sarah's answer

Utilitarianism is an ethical theory based on certain key principles such as democracy and hedonism. Bentham is credited with the initial formulation of Utilitarianism in which he demonstrated that humans were under the governance of two sovereign masters: pleasure and pain. He used this belief to develop an ethical theory which sought to maximise pleasure not for the individual but for the majority, thus producing a socially democratic ethical theory. Bentham sought to give clarification through the Hedonic Calculus, which was devised in order to measure how much pleasure was being gained, how intense it was, how long it lasted and who gained from it.

However, Bentham's idea had many criticisms and these were picked up by the other major exponent of Utilitarianism, J S Mill. Mill saw that Bentham's ideas would allow any number of appalling acts if they made the majority happy. This could lead to gang rape or torture if more people gained happiness from it. Mill therefore developed a new form of Utilitarianism which focused on higher pleasures of the mind rather than pleasures of the body, thus countering problems such as gang rape.

Examiner's tips

Always read the question: lots of questions have asked for the strengths and weaknesses of Utilitarianism or ask for an evaluation or comparison of particular parts of Utilitarianism. What ever you do, don't just write down a general description of Utilitarianism, no matter how good it is. If the question asks for the main strengths of a particular aspect of Utilitarianism you need to give the main strengths of that aspect of Utilitarianism.

If a question asks for strengths, some students give both strengths and weaknesses. This can work if the weaknesses are used to highlight where the strengths of the theory lie. However, this is quite a complex route to take in the exam. Simplicity and accuracy are often a better way forward.

If for example, there was a question asking you to explain the main strengths of one form of Utilitarianism, you need to clearly explain the principles of that form of Utilitarianism and then explain why these aspects constitute a strength. Just explaining the key features will not be sufficient to answer the question.

For example, it could be the principle of utility or the Hedonic Calculus, or you might need to say that it is devised to promote democracy and happiness. You might include the fact that Utilitarianism is straightforward and based on the desire to maximise pleasure and happiness for most people: its strength here is that it is democratic.

ExamCafé

Relax, refresh, result!

Relax and prepare

Hot tips

Religious ethics

Jermaine

I find religious ethics questions really hard – I just don't know where to start in answering them! There are so many different ideas and beliefs I never know where to begin.

Ishmall

I found the best way to approach religious ethics is to choose a specific aspect of Islam and answer questions just from that perspective. I found it hard to write criticisms of Islamic ethical theories, though.

Steve

I found that sticking to Catholic ideas was better than trying to cover all of Christianity. It also meant that I could discuss Natural Law from a religious perspective and from an ethical point of view.

Dave

Knowing the idea of the Divine Command theory and the Euthyphro dilemma really helped me discuss this topic. I found that doing Venn diagrams really helped: comparing religious ethics to other ethical theories and ideas such as absolute and relative.

Refresh your memory

Revision checklist for Religious ethics

In order to do well in this topic you will need to demonstrate knowledge and understanding of:

▷ The main ethical principles of the religion studied.
▷ How the followers of that religion make ethical decisions.
▷ The ways in which religion and morality may seem to be linked or be seen as separate from each other.
▷ How far morality may be seen as dependent on God (Divine Command theory).
▷ How far religious ethics may be seen as absolutist or relativist.
▷ How ethical theories may be considered religious.

You should also be able to discuss critically these issues and their strengths and weaknesses.

Get the result!

The general topic of this essay is outlining the main ethical principles of a religion. The candidate has chosen to answer from a Christian perspective.

Amelia's essay:

Christian ethics derive primarily from God. Many Christians believe that they can discover their ethical principles in three different ways. Firstly, through the Bible, secondly, by following Natural Law and thirdly, by listening to their conscience.

The Bible teaches Christians a number of rules which are considered to have originated from God. In the Old Testament there are 635 rules, which include the Ten Commandments. These are absolute rules which govern both how we should treat each other, e.g. 'do not kill', and how we should respond to God, e.g. 'remember the Sabbath and keep it holy'. These rules are seen by many Christians to be too specific and therefore of no use in the modern world, especially laws condemning homosexuality, whilst others still hold rules such as the Ten Commandments in highest regard.

In the New Testament the majority of Jesus' ethical teachings are found in the Sermon on the Mount. The Sermon starts with restating the Jewish laws then the Beatitudes. The main element is the Golden Rule which asks people to treat others as they would like to be treated. This has more resonance for Christians today because this can be taken in a more relativistic sense and applied to varying situations.

The main emphasis of the Bible is that ethical behaviour is an essential part of a Christian's relationship with God and therefore ethics and ethical behaviour cannot be separated from any other religious practice.

Ethical theories such as Natural Law are also important to Christians because they give clear and precise guidelines for how a Christian should behave. St Thomas Aquinas established Natural Law in the thirteenth century and started with the postulate that humans should do good and avoid evil. This dictate comes directly from God. From this, Aquinas suggested that we can use our reason to determine the correct way to behave. He developed the idea of primary and secondary precepts to help explain his ideas more fully. He also contributed to the ideas surrounding Situation Ethics, but this is a Protestant ethic.

The last way a Christian can discover what their ethical duty is, is to use their conscience. Many Christian scholars, such as Newman, have suggested that the conscience is the direct voice of God talking to them and telling them what to do. H.P Owen contributed to this suggesting that we 'cannot think of a command without thinking of the commander.'

To conclude, a Christian's ethical principles can come from the Bible, ethical theories such as Natural Law or their conscience.

If God gave us the power of **reason**, didn't he intend us to use it to make **medical** advances?

In this chapter you will learn how to apply ethical theories to:

■ the different issues raised by abortion and whether a child is a right or a gift

■ the 'sanctity of life' concept, the 'quality of life' argument and the right to euthanasia

■ genetic engineering and the ethical implications of its use

■ the concept of war and pacifism and evaluate the principles of Just War.

If God gave us the power
of **reason**, didn't he
intend us to use it to make
medical advances?

6.1 What is so special about a human being?

In this topic you will consider what is meant by the sanctity of life and by personhood.

Sanctity of life

The phrase 'sanctity of life' is used by many religious believers when talking about human life. They use it to mean that life is God-given, conferring on it a special status and making human life sacred and worthy of the highest respect. That means efforts must be made to preserve human life and its destruction is wrong.

Many biblical passages support the Christian belief in the sanctity of life. Among them is Genesis 1:27, where it states: 'God created human beings making them to be like himself.' If humans are made like God, then harming them is like harming God. Other biblical writings like Job

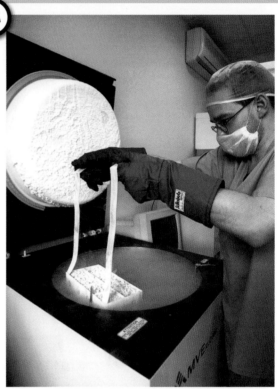

▌ Frozen embryos are inspected in the laboratory. Do you consider an embryo to be a person? What implications does your decision have for the way these embryos are treated?

1:21 state: 'I was born with nothing, and I will die with nothing. The Lord gave, and the Lord now has taken away.' For Christians, this is a clear statement that God alone has the power to create and to end life. For humans to intervene in such matters is wrong and is an attempt to 'play at being God.'

Defining exactly whose life is sanctified

Although the Ten Commandments contain the clear absolutist statement, 'You must not kill', it obviously does not mean all life created by God is protected. If that were so, what would humans eat? It is also evident that although most societies' legal codes contain a clause that says 'do not kill people' exceptions are made when it comes to warfare and capital punishment.

What makes a human being a person?

When debating issues relating to abortion and euthanasia, it is essential to define what we mean by a person. From the examples you debated or your responses to the photograph, it was evident that not everyone regarded being human and being a person as exactly the same thing. Whilst the life of a person demands respect, some have disputed whether the same rights are applicable to human tissue.

Personhood

Various people have attempted to clarify what actually constitutes a 'person' and these are some of the characteristics that have been considered.

- **Being capable of rational thought** The ability to solve problems using the power of reason distinguishes humans from animals or from human tissue grown in the laboratory. Whilst a newborn baby is not a rational individual, it does have the potential to develop rational thought. The difficulty might arise with the status of a severely handicapped adult.

- **Having a form of consciousness that enables them to feel pain or pleasure.** This criterion is certainly wide enough to include newborn babies, well-developed foetuses and severely handicapped adults. The problem is that it would also include animals.

- **Self-awareness** This means that the individual knows they belong to society, has a sense of their own identity and is aware of the past. It is not thought that animals have this sort of awareness, but neither do babies or some severely handicapped adults.

- **Having human genetic make-up** This is certainly wide enough to include babies and adults but also would include human tissue, which some might not want to accord full human rights to.

- **Being able to survive independently as a human** This definition would clarify the status of a foetus or human tissue but is open to question when a person is dependent on kidney dialysis or some other medical support for their life. It has also been pointed out that a baby can only survive with adult support.

Quality of life versus the sanctity of life

Peter Singer is one of the modern philosophers who has suggested it would be more helpful to focus on the quality of life rather than the sanctity of life when making life and death decisions.

This would move judgements from absolutist to relativist. It enables the amount of pain involved, the imminence of death and whether life holds any pleasure for the individual to be taken into consideration.

FOR DEBATE A02 skills

'All human life deserves the same respect as a person.' Look at the examples below and decide what you think. Give reasons to support your argument.

A frozen embryo; a sample of human tissue grown in the lab; a baby born without a brain.

ACTIVITY A01 skills

Consider whether a human being and a person are the same thing. Then write your own definition of a person so it is clear whose life you regard deserving of special respect.

STRETCH & CHALLENGE A01 skills

Choose one of these modern philosophers and find out what their definition of personhood is. Either Mary Anne Warren or Judith Jarvis Thomson.

What were the strengths and weaknesses of her criteria? A02 skills

6.2 The ethics of abortion

In this topic you will investigate the right to life when applied to abortion.

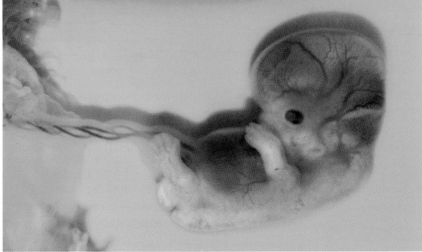

❚ Do you call this foetus a baby or a cluster of developing cells? What implications does your decision have for its right to life?

Pro-life or pro-choice?

These are two groups with opposing views on abortion. Their names sum up the different approaches they take to this subject: the right to life and the right to have a choice. Interestingly both groups accept that people have a right to life and that life is special and valuable, where they differ is whose life they are considering.

Pro-life

Even amongst those against abortion there is a spectrum of opinion ranging from the absolute stance that forbids abortion totally whatever the circumstances, to those who are prepared to accept it reluctantly under certain circumstances. Pro-life supporters argue that a foetus is a human life from the moment of conception because it contains the total blue-print for a person. The extent to which the foetus can be classed as a person was raised on pages 138–139. The question you might ask is whether a potential life is of the same value as an actual life. The Catholic Church has issued many official statements banning abortion:

> Direct abortion, that is to say, abortion willed either as an end or a means, is gravely contrary to the moral law.

When is a foetus a person?

Here are some of the stages in a foetus' development when personhood might be claimed, which would give the foetus its right to life.

- At conception – this case is supported by the fact that from the moment of fertilisation, genetically the egg contains everything that will make it a unique individual.

- At some stage during development – various stages have been suggested, i.e. from the moment when a mother feels foetal movements; the stage at which the foetus can feel pain; the stage at which a foetus can survive outside of the womb; the moment when the soul enters the foetus.

- Birth – when it can lead a life independent of its mother.

The pro-choice case

The pro-choice argument hinges on the fact that women are denied their basic human rights if they are not permitted to make decisions about their own bodies. Pro-choice supporters say that a foetus is only a potential human, and having potential is not a valid argument because it could be argued everyone has the potential to be an astronaut, but few will achieve that. The mother is an actual person and so her rights must take precedence over a potential life.

Doctrine of double effect

This doctrine accepts that abortion may occur as a result of a different medical procedure. For example, if a pregnant woman had a cancer that required the removal of her womb, the operation to save her life would necessarily mean the loss of her unborn child. Similarly a woman suffering an ectopic pregnancy (where the embryo is developing outside of the womb) would need an operation to remove the foetus or she would die. Many people accept the abortion of a foetus in situations like these because abortion was not the intention of the medical procedure, but a secondary effect.

FOR DEBATE

Who has the right to life? The mother or the child?

FURTHER RESEARCH

Use the internet to investigate the arguments put forward by a Pro-Life group and a Pro-Choice group. Design a flier for one of these groups setting out their position and pointing out the weaknesses in the opposition's case.

ACTIVITY

What ethical argument underpins the Catholic statement on page 140?

FOR DEBATE

Who else has rights to be considered in abortion cases besides the foetus and the mother? The father? Grandparents? The medical team required to carry out an abortion?

ACTIVITY

What ethical issues do these cases raise?

- A woman wants an abortion because of incest.
- A woman wants an abortion because she has bought a designer wedding dress for the big day.
- A mother wants her mentally handicapped daughter to have an abortion.

STRETCH & CHALLENGE

Find out the connection between Judith Jarvis Thomson's story of the famous violinist and abortion. Role-play, or script, an interview between Ms Thomson and a Roman Catholic about abortion.

6.3 Is a baby a gift or a right?

In this topic you will examine the issues surrounding infertility and a couple's right to a child.

ACTIVITY

Make sure that you understand the procedures for IVF, AIH (artificial insemination by husband) and AID (artificial insemination by donor). What is involved in surrogacy? There will not be any exam questions on these procedures but you need the information to write a well-argued answer.

FOR DEBATE

Infertility is an illness like any other. Everybody is entitled to free treatment including the woman in the picture.

STRETCH & CHALLENGE

Explore the difference in meaning between a gift and a right. Produce a PowerPoint presentation for the group.

❚ Advanced fertility treatment enabled this elderly woman to give birth to a baby. Is it every woman's right to give birth to a child?

Do people have a right to have children?

Article 16 of the Universal Declaration of Human Rights says:

> *Men and **women** of **full age**, without any **limitation due** to **race**, **nationality** or **religion**, have the **right** to marry and to found a **family**.*

It could be argued that this gives everyone the right to have children, though some might say that was a misinterpretation of article 16. Some might point out that the statement links marriage to having children, which might influence a person's right to a child. If the declaration gives men and women the right to parenthood, does it mean if they are infertile, they are entitled to receive treatment?

A child is a gift

Those who argue there is no entitlement to a baby point out that children are not a commodity such as a house. The religious belief that a baby is a gift from God makes God the arbiter of whether a person can have a baby or not. As a development of that, it might be argued that perhaps God does not intend some people to become parents.

A non-religious, or even a religious person might argue that infertility is nature's way of keeping the population in check, because life on our planet would be unsustainable if everybody reproduced. Others point out that fertility treatment is a recent innovation, so how can parenthood be a basic human right if the technology never existed in the past?

A child is a right

It can be argued that reproduction is a basic human instinct and women who cannot have children experience real psychological suffering. Assisting infertile couples to have a baby is simply correcting a malfunction, like performing a heart by-pass which few would doubt was a right. If advances in medicine result from the application of human reason, then they are a God-given method of helping others.

Rights and responsibilities

When talking of rights it is worth giving some thought to whose rights we are considering. The woman on the left considered that she had the right to a child. Does her child have the right to expect his/her mother to be there for them when they start secondary school and graduate from college? Indeed, does his/her mother have any responsibility to the child she gave birth to?

Does a child have a right to know who he/she is? In the case of the 64-year-old who gave birth to a child as a result of her husband's sperm and her niece's egg being fertilised and implanted, there may be an identity crisis.

IVF

When the first successful IVF treatment was reported there was widespread fear about where it might lead and tabloids ran stories about 'Frankenstein babies'. However, Louise Brown, the world's first test-tube baby, born in 1978 has grown up to be a normal, healthy young woman and many thousands of children have followed. IVF is now a widely used treatment for childless couples. The procedure still raises ethical questions and not everyone believes it is morally acceptable.

What ethical issues surround IVF?

Both the creation and the destruction of embryos involved in IVF raises ethical questions. Many people are unsure of the morality of artificially making a baby in the laboratory. You might also consider the different implications of using sperm from the husband, the lover or an unknown donor. Some might argue that using the last two donors constitutes adultery.

Because IVF procedures are not immediately successful many fertilised embryo have to be prepared. Those that are not needed are destroyed. This returns us to considering sanctity of life issues and what constitutes a person. Unwanted embryos are also valuable for use in medical research but is that acceptable?

ACTIVITY *A02 skills*

Set up a committee of three or four to consider whether the health authority can spend its limited resources on any of these cases. You need to justify your decision on ethical grounds referring to one of the ethical theories you have studied.

- You are asked to freeze a couple's embryos so the woman is free to have her career first and come to motherhood when she chooses, even if she is past the menopause.
- A couple in a civil partnership claim their right to a child and access to treatment the same as a heterosexual couple.
- A woman who is 56 wants fertility treatment in order to have a baby with her new husband.

ACTIVITY *A01 skills*

Using the work you did on the status of the foetus and personhood (pages 138–139) produce a brief report on the ethical implications of IVF treatment for a hospital laboratory.

ACTIVITY *A01 skills*

Make a diagram, or an ideas map, exploring the implications of the right to a child.

6.4 How do ethical theories apply to abortion and the right to a child?

In this topic you will study the application and approach of Utilitarianism, Natural Law, Kantian ethics and Christian ethics to abortion and the right to a child.

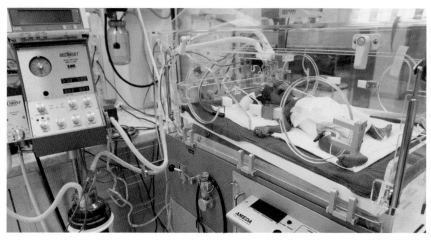

▌ This baby has a serious medical problem that means it will have a very short life involving intrusive and expensive medical procedures. Would it have been right to have aborted it at an early stage in pregnancy? Apply one of the ethical theories below to this case.

ACTIVITY A01 skills

Write a web page for a Utilitarian website giving their views on the morality of abortion.

STRETCH & CHALLENGE A01 skills

How do you think Kant would have responded to women asking him whether IVF was an acceptable fertility treatment? How would he have supported his argument?

Natural Law

Aquinas' Natural Law philosophy (see pages 102–103) has as a Primary Precept 'the preservation of life'. This absolute theory permits no exceptions, so the life of the unborn is given the same status as an existing life and abortion also goes against the natural purpose of conception. IVF is totally unacceptable to followers of Natural Law because it intrudes into the natural process of conception and involves the destruction of lives in the form of unwanted embryos. All artificial methods of helping a woman to conceive are rejected because they involve masturbation to create sperm, which is regarded as misuse of the genitalia.

Because Natural Law is concerned with the motive and not the outcome of an action there is an acceptance of the doctrine of Double Effect (see pages 141). Roman Catholic Christianity is based on Natural Law and this extract from the Catholic Encyclopaedia explains the position.

If medical treatment or surgical operation, necessary to save a mother's life, is applied to her organism (though the child's death would, or at least might, follow as a regretted but unavoidable consequence), it should not be maintained that the foetal life is thereby directly attacked.

Utilitarianism

Because this philosophy is concerned with outcome, it weighs up the happiness and pain of all involved. That includes foetus, mother and indeed everybody, whether family or medical staff. By focusing on the outcome of an action Utilitarians are rejecting the argument that life has an intrinsic value.

When Utilitarianism is applied to a woman's right to a child the same balancing of pleasure against pain takes place. Other factors for consideration might be the cost of the treatment and whether the same money might bring more happiness if used differently.

Decisions about the morality of IVF also involve weighing up the pain caused to the embryos that are destroyed against the pleasure provided by a successful pregnancy.

Kantian ethics

An important part of Kant's philosophy is that people should be treated as ends in themselves and not means. This has clear implications for abortion if the foetus is considered a person. If the foetus is not considered to be a reasoning individual, then abortion could be acceptable. However, a mother who has an abortion in order to be free to get on with her own life would be judged to be wrong according to Kantian ethics.

Since Kant requires principles to be universalised it is difficult to rule on abortion because there are many different situations.

Christian ethics

Not only do Christians believe in the sanctity of life but they also regard a child as God's gift of love to a couple. This belief underpins their views about abortion and the right of humans to intervene when God has not given them a child. Because Christian marriage is a sacred union in which sexual relations exist to produce children, some would say fertility treatment has no part in God's plan and is wrong.

The Roman Catholic Church states:

> The embryonic child … has a human soul; and therefore is a man from the time of its conception; therefore it has an equal right to its life with its mother; therefore neither the mother, not medical practitioner, nor any human being whatever can lawfully take that life away.

Compare this with the views of the Baptists, who believe in the sanctity of life yet hold a broad range of opinions about the beginning of human life and the value attached to that life as it develops.

FURTHER RESEARCH — A01 skills

Find out what MP Mrs Jill Knight said in the abortion debate in House of Commons in 1966. How did she support her case? Write an account of her argument to give to other members of the group.

ACTIVITY — A02 skills

Read the Church of England's views on abortion:

'The Church of England combines strong opposition to abortion with a recognition that there can be – strictly limited – conditions under which it may be morally preferable to any available alternative.

'The mother of the unborn child needs all possible understanding and help, especially if factors connected with the pregnancy are difficult. It is the mother who is pregnant, it is she who will have to agree to an abortion if that proves necessary … Her feelings and wishes are to be fully recognised. At the same time sight should not be lost of the father's proper role and responsibilities in decision making concerning the child.'

How does their approach to abortion differ from that of Natural Law, which underpins the Catholic view?

6.5 News stories

In this topic you will look at some recent real-life news stories and consider the ethical issues they raise.

New mother, 66, says giving birth was her mission in life

A 66-year-old mother believed to be the oldest woman to give birth has dismissed concerns that she is too old to rear the child.

Adriana Iliescu told reporters in Bucharest that the baby was her mission in life, at a press conference held 48 hours after the 3lb 3oz baby girl was delivered by Caesarean section.

"You don't have to be concerned," said Miss Iliescu, who is a single mother. "(The baby's future) is my concern." She added, smiling, that the girl "will have a beautiful future".

Miss Iliescu became pregnant with triplets through in vitro fertilization using sperm and egg from anonymous donors, after nine years of fertility treatment failed to help her to conceive. One foetus died at ten weeks. After a second foetus died in the womb earlier this month, weighing just 1lb 8oz, doctors induced the birth five weeks early.

Despite the fact that she is not genetically related to her daughter, Miss Iliescu said that the baby looked like her.

"Each person has a mission on earth. My mission was to prove that women who want to have children can do it," the new mother said at the news conference at the Giulesti Maternity Hospital in the Romanian capital. She added that she had an "out of this world feeling" when she touched the baby's fingers for the first time yesterday.

"Today is a happy day for me, because I can see my daughter. I have touched her hand and she squeezed my finger," she said at the press conference at the Giulesti maternity hospital in Bucharest.

"It is completely different from when you touch someone else's child. I was very happy that she took my finger."

Miss Iliescu, a retired university professor in literature and a writer of children's books, said that she hoped the girl would follow in her steps and become a literature teacher.

© Jenny Booth, 19 January 2005

Man, 72, to be sperm donor for son and daughter-in-law

A 72-year-old man has agreed to donate his sperm to his son and daughter-in-law after the London couple were unable to conceive a child through IVF.

Dr Peter Bowen-Simkins, the clinic's co-medical director, told the newspaper that he had never come across a case like this before. But advancements in fertility treatment meant that people were now willing to consider all kinds of options.

He said: "Obviously the wife's mother-in-law also had to be included in all the conversations but she has no objections. Society has also changed its perceptions of what is and what is not acceptable. "In this case, keeping the identity of the child similar to their own was a huge factor. The husband does not have a brother, which is why he chose his own father to assist."

Any baby produced from the treatment would be the grandfather's genetic child and its father's half-brother.

© Jane Kirby, 6 October 2007

Babies aborted for minor disabilities

MORE than 50 babies with club feet were aborted in just one area of England in a three-year period, according to new statistics. Thirty-seven babies with cleft lips or palates and 26 with extra or webbed fingers or toes were also aborted.

This has raised concerns about abortions being carried out for minor disabilities that could be cured by surgery.

Abortions are allowed up to birth in Britain in cases of serious handicap, but the law does not define what conditions should be considered grave Enough to allow a termination late in the pregnancy. That is left to the discretion of doctors. The Commons science and technology committee is carrying out an inquiry into whether the law should be made more specific.

Some parents, doctors and campaign groups are worried by what they see as a tendency to stretch the definition of serious handicap. In 2003 Joanna Jepson, a Church of England curate, instigated a legal challenge against West Mercia police for failing to prosecute doctors who carried out an abortion on a baby with a cleft palate at 28 weeks' gestation. The challenge failed but raised public concerns over terminations for minor disabilities.

However, the latest figures — released by the South West Congenital Anomaly Register show that dozens of abortions are still carried out after the condition is discovered.

Jepson, now vicar of St Peter's church in Fulham, west London, said: "These figures raise grave questions about how the law is being implemented for babies diagnosed with a disability. I have strong doubts that the law is being used to protect the unborn."

Julia Millington, political director of the ProLife Alliance,added: "It is incomprehensible that a baby would be rejected for what amounts to little more than a cosmetic imperfection. Equality for the disabled cannot be achieved until we remove this discriminatory provision in the law." The figures record abortions for congenital anomalies in southwest England from Cornwall to Wiltshire between 2002 and 2005. They show that 54 babies with club feet, 16 with extra or webbed fingers and 10 with extra or webbed toes were aborted. The stage at which the abortions were carried out was not recorded, but the abnormalities would have been diagnosed at about 20 weeks' gestation.

© Sarah-Kate Templeton, 21 October 2007

Applied ethics

6.6 Euthanasia

In this topic you will consider the ethical issues raised by euthanasia.

KEYWORD

Euthanasia involves assisting a person to die to spare them suffering.

❚ Many people would argue if your dog reaches this stage it is your duty as a responsible pet-owner to have it put to sleep. What is the reasoning behind that assumption? Why doesn't the same hold true for one of your relatives?

What do we mean by euthanasia?

Euthanasia literally means 'a good death', but euthanasia is also called 'mercy killing.' The idea behind both names is that a person should be permitted or assisted to die, to spare them further suffering. The suffering may take the form of physical pain or mental suffering from a debilitating disease that entails loss of dignity and total dependence on someone else.

Euthanasia is illegal in Britain and most countries. However, the Netherlands legalised euthanasia in 2001 according to very strict criteria, while Switzerland permits a doctor to assist suicide. The legalisation of euthanasia remains a hotly debated topic as advances in medical technology can extend the life-span of patients but not necessarily the quality of life.

ACTIVITY

A02 skills

What would be the advantage of having an absolute code on euthanasia? What are the advantages of a relativist code? Both approaches have their weaknesses. What are they?

Active and passive euthanasia

Euthanasia can broadly be divided into two categories.

1. One involves the patient asking for help to end their life. This is voluntary euthanasia (also called active euthanasia) and a form of assisted suicide which might arise when a patient's life became unbearable but they were not in a position to end it themselves. They might seek the assistance of a family member or ask a doctor to administer a lethal injection to end their suffering.

2. Involuntary euthanasia occurs when someone else judges a person's quality of life is so poor, it would be kinder to end their life rather than let them continue suffering. The dog in the picture faces involuntary

euthanasia. Involuntary euthanasia might be considered for a human who was comatose or in a persistent vegetative state (PVS) – where they are kept alive solely by a machine, unable to respond to any outside stimulus nor likely to recover. They might be referred to as 'brain dead'. Involuntary euthanasia can also be called passive euthanasia.

Involuntary euthanasia is also used to describe a situation where a patient's life has been ended because someone has deliberately chosen *not* to give life-saving treatment.

Sanctity of life

Remind yourself of the arguments about the sanctity of life on page 138. Obviously they apply as much to discussions about euthanasia as they did to abortion. Whilst most societies state that killing is wrong, we know that exceptions are made to this rule in time of war and for capital punishment.

If life is sacred, because it is a gift from God, there is also the understanding that God has power to end life. When humans intervene to end life, whether it be their own or another person's, they are going against the will of God. As with abortion, the sanctity of life means taking life is totally wrong. Once again it is the contentious area of personhood that makes it difficult to apply the sanctity of life.

Personhood and quality of life

As with discussions about abortion, an important consideration in this debate is at what point a human ceases to be a person. Much of this will hinge on their quality of life.

You might argue that the patient who has been pronounced 'brain-dead' is no longer a person. If they were being kept alive by a life-support machine we would certainly recognise them as human. However, if their condition is such that they have no reactions and are totally incapable of independent thought we may no longer consider them a person. The problem of course is that a severely mentally disabled person or one suffering paralysis may also exhibit similar tendencies or lack of them. Are they still considered to be a real person? Look back to the criteria on page 139.

Suffering has a purpose

Not only are Christians convinced that all life is sacred, many also believe that God may well have a purpose for suffering. You can probably think of cases yourself where someone has come through a difficult situation a much stronger character as a result of their experiences. Some Christians also regard suffering as a test of faith. Others see it is a punishment for disobeying God's rules and once that person repents, their suffering ends. Since Jesus suffered on the cross to save humanity, there is also the understanding amongst Christians that human suffering enables them to draw closer to Jesus. If suffering has a purpose, then humans have no right to intervene and that removes the case for euthanasia.

FOR DEBATE

'The sanctity of life makes euthanasia absolutely wrong for Christians.' Should decisions about euthanasia be based on the sanctity of life, or love?

ACTIVITY

Read the case of Dr Nigel Cox, the only British doctor convicted of attempting to perform euthanasia.

In 1991, 70-year-old Lillian Boyes was dying of rheumatoid arthritis in great pain. She asked her doctor to assist her to die but he refused. All he would do was administer painkillers. She then told him she wanted no further treatment. In the final hours of her life, the pain was so agonising Dr Cox administered a lethal injection to enable her to die peacefully. Because it could not be proved conclusively that the injection had actually killed Lillian Boyes, the doctor was charged with attempted murder, rather than murder.

ACTIVITY

Do you agree with what:

- Lillian Boyes did?
- The doctor did?
- The judge did?

Applied ethics

6.7 When is a life no longer a life?

In this topic you will examine arguments about the quality of life in relation to euthanasia.

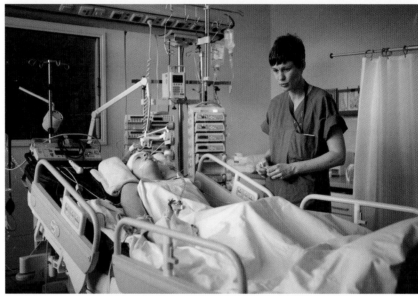

▌ This person is on a life-support machine. If you were a doctor, would you ever consider switching life-support off? What are you basing your decision on?

Life and death decisions

Many ethical decisions about euthanasia hinge on whether the human being in question can be considered to be a 'person'. With abortion, personhood was concerned with stages of development; with euthanasia it is concerned with stages of dying. It could be argued that a human is a person until they are dead. However, others have argued that euthanasia involves humans who are already dying and are sliding further away from being a person. Whilst that might be easy to understand in the case of the person in the picture, who is totally dependent on life-support, shows no responses and is not expected to make any recovery, the stages in between this are less clear-cut. Furthermore, with the continual progress of medicine, who can say with any certainty that recovery will be impossible?

The quality of life

Associated with the debate about personhood when deciding life and death matters, is the consideration of someone's quality of life. What people usually mean by this is not just freedom from pain but also retaining control over their life and their self-respect. In some cases when a person feels they have lost everything that makes their life worthwhile, they end their life. Sad though this is, suicide is not illegal. Supporters of euthanasia argue that it should be regarded as assisted suicide, and a doctor should be allowed to help a terminally ill patient who feels their life is no longer worth living but is not in a position to end it themselves.

The case of Diane Pretty's human rights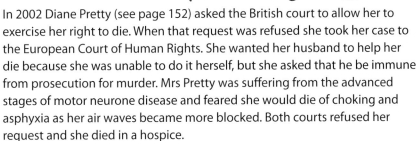

In 2002 Diane Pretty (see page 152) asked the British court to allow her to exercise her right to die. When that request was refused she took her case to the European Court of Human Rights. She wanted her husband to help her die because she was unable to do it herself, but she asked that he be immune from prosecution for murder. Mrs Pretty was suffering from the advanced stages of motor neurone disease and feared she would die of choking and asphyxia as her air waves became more blocked. Both courts refused her request and she died in a hospice.

The slippery slope

When people talk of the slippery slope, they are considering relativist solutions to euthanasia which will allow individual judgements to be made in each situation. In the case of euthanasia, some might argue that an absolutist ethical code is the only safe approach: a view most countries in the world share. The fear is that if any form of euthanasia is permitted it would open the floodgates to removing inconvenient members of society. This would devalue human life.

Once killing a person is sanctioned, for whatever reason, some people think it is not such a big step for society to permit the removal of other categories of people. Some people cite the example of the Nazis who killed thousands of gypsies, disabled people and homosexuals as well as Jews. This is not the best example of the 'slippery slope' in operation because the Nazis did not accidentally slide into this position; it was a far more deliberate decision.

It is worth pointing out that there is no evidence from The Netherlands, where euthanasia is permitted, that the slippery slope has occurred.

Abuse of the system

Another reason why people object to legalising euthanasia is because people might abuse the system or feel pressured into asking for death. If voluntary euthanasia were permitted an elderly relative who needed expensive nursing care might feel they ought not to be an emotional and financial burden on their family and so request death. It is also possible that unscrupulous family members with their sights on a large inheritance might put pressure on their elderly relatives to request euthanasia. Similar pressure might be felt by the parents of a severely disabled child whose care would cost the local authority huge sums of money.

6.8 The right to life or the right to death?

In this topic you will consider what people mean by having the right to life and whether a person has the right to choose the time and manner of their death.

▌ Diane Pretty believed that people did have the right to choose how and when they died. She battled through the courts for this right but was defeated. Her story appears on page 151.

The right to die

Whilst abortion is predominantly concerned with the right to life, euthanasia is concerned with the right to die. Some people argue it is their life, so only they have the right to decide when, and how, it should end. The legalisation of suicide in 1961 recognised that people do have that right, but others argue whilst we have a right to die, we do not have a right to be killed, nor to ask someone to kill us.

A living will

A few people choose to write a living will or an Advance Directive in which they say exactly what treatment they would like to receive in the event of them becoming so ill or injured they cannot communicate their wishes. This might include the wish not to be revived if severely brain-damaged, or not to be kept alive by life-support once brain-dead. Whilst this restores a person's autonomy, this document has no legal status and a doctor might decide the living will was not in the patient's best interests.

ACTIVITY A02 skills

What would be the grounds for treating euthanasia in a different way to suicide?
Do you agree?

FOR DEBATE A02 skills

It is the duty of a doctor to attempt to prolong life.

The right to life

Not everyone believes that a terminally ill patient should consider euthanasia as the only option. The hospice movement, founded by Cicely Saunders, a Christian, offers pain control, palliative care and a dignified end to a person's natural life. There is a concern that if euthanasia were legalised, it would put pressure on vulnerable people, such as those who are disabled or elderly, to request euthanasia for the sake of their family.

How do people who are unable to speak for themselves make a decision, or transmit their decision, about life and death issues? Not only is there the person in a coma to consider, there is the severely handicapped newborn baby rejected by her parents to consider. It could be argued that a disabled baby ought to be permitted to live so that it can exercise its own judgement on the value of its life when it is old enough, rather than surrender those rights to others at birth.

Do doctors have a duty to carry out a patient's wishes?

Certainly a doctor has a duty to obey a patient's request that they receive no further treatment even if the doctor knows that lack of treatment would bring about the patient's death. However, at the start of a medical career, doctors swear an oath to heal and not to end life.

Does society have a right to make decisions on these people's behalf?

Case Study 1

In 2002 Miss B took her case to the British High Court by video link. The 43-year-old woman was paralysed from the neck down and kept alive on a ventilator. She asked permission for the doctors to withdraw her treatment by switching off the ventilator. Dame Elizabeth Butler-Sloss ruled that Miss B had the 'necessary mental capacity to give consent or to refuse consent to life-sustaining medical treatment', and gave permission for Miss B to be transferred to another hospital where she could receive the treatment she wished and care to 'ease her suffering and permit her life to end peacefully and with dignity.'

Case Study 2

In 1997 Annie Lindsell petitioned the High Court for permission for her doctor to administer the drug diamorphine should she begin suffocating or choking to death during the final stages of her motor neurone disease. This drug would end her life. The case was withdrawn when Ms Lindsell was informed that her doctor could legally administer the drug to relieve her mental or physical distress.

What was the implication of this new information?

STRETCH & CHALLENGE · A01 skills

What is the Hippocratic oath? What is its relevance to abortion and to euthanasia?

ACTIVITY · A02 skills

Analyse the case of Miss B, which made legal history, in terms of what ethical judgments were made and whether the death of Miss B constituted euthanasia or not. Why do you think did the court not permit Diane Pretty permission to die, when she was exactly the same age as Miss B and also felt herself trapped in a useless body?

ACTIVITY · A02 skills

Examine this case of Annie Lindsell from the perspective of euthanasia and explain the ethical reasons why her doctor was permitted to administer a life-shortening drug.

Applied ethics

6.9 Applying ethical theories to the arguments about euthanasia

In this topic you will consider the way Natural Law, Kantian ethics, Utilitarianism and Christian ethics react to euthanasia.

 People support the hospice by buying from this charity shop. This particular hospice offers pain relief and palliative treatment to children suffering from a terminal illness. The needs of parents and family are also considered in this environment. Which ethical theory would agree with the hospice as an alternative to euthanasia and which would not?

ACTIVITY A02 skills

Consider the example of a mother who has given birth to a very weak and severely disabled baby. Doctors say that the baby will have a short life that is likely to involve pain. Should the doctors put the baby on life-support and make every effort to preserve its life? Should they give the baby painkillers which they know will shorten its life or should they withhold all treatment knowing it will die naturally?

Try applying the Hedonic Calculus to this situation. Is that a helpful way of arriving at an ethical decision? Was the outcome one that you thought was correct?

Natural Law

Remind yourself of the basic tenets of this philosophy on pages 98–103. Supporters of Natural Law look to Aquinas' First Primary Precept, the preservation of life, to guide their response to euthanasia. Natural Law also draws on our innate sense of what is right and what is wrong, which leads supporters of this philosophy to assert that we all know taking life is wrong. It is wrong to take our own life and wrong to ask others to do it for us. The right response would be to allow nature to take its course and for death to occur in its own time.

This would also make it wrong to intervene with drugs or any other treatment that could alleviate pain or reduce suffering. Such a philosophy would also permit a policy of leaving severely handicapped infants to die.

Kantian ethics

Remind yourself of this philosophy on pages 104–109. A key part of Kantian ethics is that a person must be treated as an end and not a means, which means euthanasia could only be considered if the individual, and not society or the family, benefited from the action. It is also necessary for the person making the judgement to be able to reason. That immediately prohibits involuntary euthanasia.

Kant also said all actions must arise from a sense of duty and he looked to the moral law within us to find that duty. Moral law would tell us that it is wrong to take life and it is our duty to preserve it, making euthanasia wrong.

Applying Kant's formulation of universality to euthanasia might permit active euthanasia because it is possible to argue a person in full possession of their reasoning powers, but terminally ill, might want to end their suffering.

Kantian ethics requires objective, unemotional judgements which are virtually impossible with decisions about euthanasia.

Utilitarianism

Familiarise yourself with this argument on pages 110–113. By focusing on the consequences of euthanasia, Utilitarianism rejects the sanctity of life argument. It considers whether euthanasia is a good action by examining the pleasure it brings to everyone concerned.

Utilitarianism does take into account the autonomy of the individual and the benefits a patient might gain from being permitted to die with dignity.

By definition Utilitarianism will also weigh up the happiness, or benefit, of everybody else involved. That could include members of the family, friends, the medical team and even the wider implications of expenses to the health service. When they are all taken into consideration, the patient's interests are in the minority. Certainly if the cost of caring for a terminally ill person is factored into a hospital's budget, it is likely that a greater number of patients could benefit if the same money was spent elsewhere.

Christian ethics

Christians believe that life is sacred and should be protected. Deliberately accelerating a person's death at their request, or to relieve distress, goes against God's will and is wrong.

Many Christians make a distinction between killing and letting someone die. The Church of England says:

> *Doctors do not have an overriding obligation to prolong life by all available means, if to do so is also to prolong suffering.*

6.10 Genetic engineering in the news

In this topic you will look at some recent news stories about genetic engineering and consider the ethical issues they raise.

ACTIVITY **A01 skills**

Read each of these extracts and note down the ethical issues that they raise. Then choose one story and write a comment on it from the perspective of one of the ethical theories you have studied.

Designer baby couple appeal for son's life

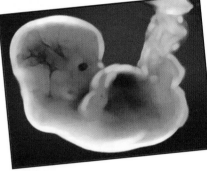

A COUPLE seeking to create Britain's first "designer baby" to provide a life-saving tissue donation for their terminally ill son say that they are losing a race against time.

Raj and Shahana Hashmi, who want to use genetic screening to have a child who could save the life of four-year-old Zain, said yesterday that their chances of success were falling with every day that permission was held up in the courts.

The couple, from Leeds, begin an appeal today against a High Court ruling in December that blocked their treatment with a tissue-typing technique. The procedure would ensure that a new sibling for Zain would have the right genetic make-up to donate stem cells from his or her umbilical cord. Zain, who suffers from the rare inherited blood disorder beta-thalassaemia, cannot make any red blood cells of his own and is kept alive by five painful 12-hour transfusions every week. He will die without a bone marrow or stem cell transplant, and no suitable donor has been found despite a worldwide search.

The Hashmis had another natural child, Harris, in the hope that he might be able to donate the tissue, but he did not turn out to be a match. New IVF techniques could be used to ensure that any future baby could donate, but a decision by the Human Fertilisation and Embryology Authority (HFEA) to approve this therapy was overturned after a legal challenge by Roman Catholic anti-abortion campaigners.

Even if the Hashmis and the HFEA win today's appeal they may have lost vital months that could make the difference between life or death for Zain. Mrs Hashmi, will be 39 this month, and her chances of a successful conception are falling all the time. Zain's transplant, too, is most likely to succeed if it takes place before he is five and a half, in 18 months. "We are aware that time is not on our side," Mr Hashmi said, "so we need a decision quickly." A ruling is expected before Easter.

Simon Fishel of the Park Hospital in Nottingham, who is treating the couple, said: "Shahana is approaching reproductive maturity and this makes it more and more difficult to achieve a pregnancy. We are probably looking at a 10 per cent chance per attempt, and this goes down very rapidly as time goes on."

© Mark Henderson, 1 April 2003

Five little piggies

Five cloned female piglets, named Noel, Angel, Star, Joy and Mary – an important step towards "knock-out pigs" – were born on Christmas Day 2001 in what the Scottish-based firm PPL Therapeutics says is a major step towards successfully producing animal organs and cells for use in human transplants.

The pigs lack a gene to which the human immune system reacts aggressively. When an all-male litter is born and bred with the females, a knock-out pig will be created.

Trees with rabbit genes accelerate cleaning of soil

Genetically modified plants that can break down pollutants may be an effective way to clean soil contaminated by industrial chemicals and explosives used by the military, according to scientists.

Tests on six-inch tall GM poplar cuttings which had a gene from a rabbit inserted into them showed that they could remove up to 91% of a chemical called trichloroethylene from the water used in their feed. This chemical, used as an industrial degreaser and one of the most common contaminants of ground water, was broken down by the plants into harmless byproducts more than 100 times faster than by unaltered plants.

"In view of their large size and extensive root systems, these transgenic poplars may provide the means to effectively clean sites contaminated with a variety of pollutants at much faster rates and at lower costs than can be achieved with current conventional techniques," wrote Sharon Doty, of the University of Washington, Seattle, yesterday in the Proceedings of the National Academy of Sciences (PNAS).

The GM poplars also broke down other common environmental pollutants such as chloroform, a byproduct of the disinfection of drinking water, the solvent carbon tetrachloride, and vinyl chloride, used to make plastics.

Poplars use an enzyme called cytochrome P450 to break down contaminants. Trichloroethylene is turned into a harmless salt, water and carbon dioxide.

After Dr Doty's team inserted the gene into the tree from a rabbit they also produced P450, but at a much faster rate. Ultimately, the scientists would like to manipulate the plant's own genes to achieve the same goal. Mammalian cytochrome P450 has been used in the past to create GM plants that can detoxify herbicidetreated fields. In 2005, Japanese scientists used a human gene to produce rice plants capable of degrading a number of herbicides.

Applied ethics

6.11 What is genetic engineering and why are people so concerned about it?

In this topic you will learn what modern science is doing in the field of genetic engineering and some of the ethical issues raised by it.

▌ This mouse was given genes from a jellyfish in order to make it fluorescent to aid research into treatments for cancer. Do you think this is an acceptable use of genetic engineering?

'It's all in the genes,' they say. But what do they mean?

People use that expression to indicate that someone is behaving in a certain way because they have inherited that characteristic from their parents. We get 50 per cent of our genes from each parent and the particular mix we have defines us as an individual. Only identical twins have the same genetic make-up.

Every living being is made up of cells and each one contains a full set of genes carried on long threads of DNA, like those you saw in the Human Genome model on page 137. Genes are the basic building blocks of life, the blueprint for each living organism.

How can genes be engineered?

It is possible to extract a single gene from a cell in the laboratory and manipulate that gene before replacing it in the cell it came from. It is also possible to put a gene into a different living organism. That means it is no longer science fiction to think of a pig with genetic material from a spider or a strawberry in its body. The process of artificially manipulating genes is called genetic engineering.

What is the advantage of genetic engineering?

By altering the genetic make-up of a plant or animal it is possible to improve specific characteristics or correct some malfunction. A fruit or vegetable plant could be genetically engineered to yield a larger crop, have a high vitamin content, or produce a fruit with a longer shelf life in the supermarket.

FOR DEBATE A02 skills

Genetic engineering goes against nature and God. It is dangerous and should be stopped.

Animals can be genetically altered to produce milk containing a certain vaccine, or to survive in colder climates or grow a suitable kidney for human transplant.

If genetic engineering is applied to humans, it could enable a scientist to locate the gene responsible for diabetes and replace it with a healthy one in that person's body.

Why are people concerned about genetic engineering?

It isn't really the idea of mad scientists doing evil experiments that concerns people, although that is certainly possible. A far greater fear concerns the creation of unnatural life forms by artificially manipulating plants and animals. The photograph on the opposite page has that element about it. Is it really right to create a glow-in-the-dark mouse even if it may help to find a cure for cancer?

Because this is such new bio-technology, no-one knows what the long-term effects are of altering the genetic make-up of a living organism. The effect on the plant or animal can be observed, but what will be the consequences if that organism reproduced or was eaten? Genetic engineering is such a recent phenomenon, there has not been time to study the long-term consequences, yet the developments continue at a pace.

What right has anyone to alter the genetic make-up of another being?

This is another fundamental ethical issue for religious and non-religious people alike. Human life is so precious, does anyone have the right to interfere with it in such a fundamental way? Is the altered person a new individual?

Genetic engineering is nothing new

Supporters of genetic engineering point out we have been selectively breeding plants and animals for hundreds of years with the same intention of improving them for our needs. Grasses have been selected and cross-pollinated since prehistoric times to get the high-yielding cereal crops we have today. Cattle too have been selected and bred to produce pedigree herds with high milk yields or good flesh for eating. People choose flowers with a sweet fragrance or a long vase life, which have only come about by selective breeding and **cloning**. Others buy pedigree dogs or cats selectively bred to strengthen certain characteristics.

Is it true? Has genetic engineering been around for years?

Not really. There is a difference between selective breeding and artificially removing genes and replacing them with others. Changes as a result of selective breeding take many years to yield results whereas gene manipulation is fast. Plant cloning has been around for years; you may have put a cutting in water to develop roots before growing it on. Cloning of animals is a very new technique, as Dolly the sheep showed (see page 162).

ACTIVITY *A02 skills*

Write a press release from a major pharmaceutical company, who have recently gained funding for genetic research, explaining why it is such a good thing.

ACTIVITY *A01 skills*

How might a Christian apply the sanctity of life belief to genetic engineering?

ACTIVITY *A01 skills*

Write an FAQ section for an RS website to explain what genetic engineering is and why it might be of interest to students of RS.

KEY WORD

Cloning: a form of genetic engineering that produces a new life that is a genetic copy of its parent.

Applied ethics

6.12 Is this Dr Frankenstein at work?

In this topic you will consider the implications of genetic engineering involving plants and animals.

❚ Experiments with GM crops in Britain in the late 1990s produced anti-GM demonstrations like this and an outcry in the tabloids. What were people frightened of?

What are GM crops?

Genetically Modified (or GM) crops are grown from a seed whose genetic make-up has been engineered to promote specific characteristics. Crop trials of GM maize were taking place in the field shown in this photograph. The seed had been genetically modified by an American multinational company to make it disease and drought-resistant and to produce a higher yield.

Why are people so concerned?

Nobody knows what the long-term health implications are for people who eat these products regularly. Might they develop illnesses or allergies? The impact on the environment is another unknown. Concerns have been raised about the effect on wildlife that eats such crops or the effect of pollen from these plants on other plants nearby, because genetically modified plants are introducing new, artificially-created material into the food chain. Although scientists have tried to isolate the fields that are trialling GM crops, creating a total exclusion zone around a field is impossible: the action of weather and birds is unpredictable. Plants will find ways of reproducing and genetically modified material might be spread into other plants, both crops and weeds. People who have spent years working towards gaining full organic status are especially concerned their efforts might be destroyed. Because genetic modification is such a new science, not enough research has been done into what diseases GM crops might be susceptible to.

Genetically engineered animals

The same **transgenic** issues apply to animals as to plants whose structures have been altered to assist humans. A cow can be genetically modified to produce milk with a human blood-clotting agent or with antibodies in it. Other animals have been engineered to develop diseases like cancer or cystic fibrosis, to enable scientists to test treatments on them.

The area which always produces hot debate is that of cloning. This involves

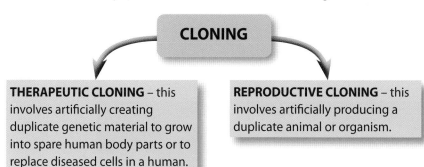

CLONING

THERAPEUTIC CLONING – this involves artificially creating duplicate genetic material to grow into spare human body parts or to replace diseased cells in a human.

REPRODUCTIVE CLONING – this involves artificially producing a duplicate animal or organism.

creating a duplicate organism, an identical copy of a plant or animal.

Dolly the Sheep

Dolly was the first and most famous example of a cloned animal. She was created in Edinburgh in 1997, when an egg cell was removed from the ovary of female sheep A. The nucleus of that egg, which contained the DNA, was removed. In its place was put the DNA from sheep B. This had been extracted from a body cell taken from sheep B. The newly formed cell was allowed to developed into an embryo and then implanted into the womb of a foster mother, sheep C. The lamb then born was a genetic clone, in other words a duplicate, of sheep B, whose DNA had been used.

The birth of Dolly the Sheep, as the lamb was nicknamed, was a breakthrough in genetic engineering and presented the possibility of cloning other animals, even humans.

Although Dolly's birth was a success story, 430 manipulated eggs had originally been produced, of those only 277 had begun developing into embryos and only 23 were viable for transplanting. Dolly was the only successful lamb: others had miscarried or suffered severe abnormalities.

Dolly herself had a short life. She had to be put to sleep at the age of six, which is half the normal life span of a sheep, because she was suffering from a progressive lung disease. Her body had aged much more quickly than expected, probably because she was cloned from the cells of a six year old adult sheep: as one scientist explained, 'Dolly was older than her body.'

6.13 What is the problem with using human embryos in genetic engineering?

In this topic you will study the impact of genetic engineering on human embryos and consider the ethical implications of this type of work.

What is different about genetically modifying an animal and a human?

In a biological sense humans are animals, but plenty of people have reservations about applying genetic engineering to humans. You will recall there were two different uses of cloning (see page 161) and, whilst some people might accept therapeutic use, more have reservations about its reproductive use.

▌ Cloning Dolly the Sheep produced fierce debate and genuine fear in some people. They were concerned if a sheep could be cloned, then why not a human. What's wrong with that?

Using stem cells

The cells in our body develop to carry out specific functions: we have brain cells, kidney cells, and so on. Stem cells, however, are at an early stage of development and have the potential to develop into different kinds of cells. Adult stems cells taken from a particular part of the body have the potential to grow into the cells of the organ they were taken from. This could be useful in medicine because an adult's stem cell could be removed, grown in the lab, then transplanted back into that same person to replace a diseased or damaged body tissue. Because the cell originally came from that person the body would not reject it.

Research with adult stem cells is not very advanced at present. This is because research has concentrated on stem cells from human embryos. These are far more versatile, with the potential to grow into any type of body cell.

SOURCES OF HUMAN STEM CELLS

ADULT STEM CELLS – all adults have some stem cells but they are not easy to collect or develop. The stem cells can only grow into cells for the organ they came from.

EMBRYO STEM CELLS – stem cells are easily collected from a five-day-old embryo; they have the potential to grow into any body cell.

CLONED EMBRYONIC CELLS – body tissue taken from a person is cloned to produce an embryo. Stem cells are taken from that embryo, which is a genetic match to the original adult.

Working with embryos

As a result of IVF treatment (see page 143), thousands of embryos are created that are not required for fertility treatment. Normally they would be destroyed. When some of these unwanted embryos are four or five days old (and still a microscopic cluster of cells), the stem cells are removed for use in therapeutic research. They can be grown in the laboratory to be developed to repair diseased tissue in people, used for drug testing or used for research into the progress of certain diseases. They remain human tissue and are never grown into humans and are destroyed when their medical use is completed.

Those opposed say:

- It is wrong to use a human being, or any part of them, in this way.

- The consequences of this sort of cloning are unknown. Deformities, viruses or cancers may well result from it. Dolly the sheep had unforeseen medical problems and died prematurely.

- A human life is sacred and should not be used in this way.

- An embryo is a human being because it already has the potential to develop into a unique person.

- This is playing God and nobody should be involved in this sort of creation.

- Beginning with cell cloning is the slippery slope to reproductive cloning, which few people think is right. Already there are rumours that some doctors abroad have cloned humans.

Those in favour say:

- Anything which benefits humanity must be good.

- At this stage an embryo is simply a cluster of cells and does not count as a human being.

- The embryos were not wanted and would have been destroyed; none are deliberately created for experimentation.

see page 143

ACTIVITY A01 skills

What medical and ethical problems might there be with utilising each of the sources in the diagram?

ACTIVITY A01 skills

Go through the points in favour and against the use of human embryos to decide which are religious arguments and which simply ethical points. Which are teleological and which deontological?

ACTIVITY A02 skills

Add your views to these messages posted on the RS chat room website.

- Don't you think an embryo is a real person?
- OK, human life is special but when does it actually begin?
- Doesn't embryonic research treat human life like a consumer item and just discard the packaging?
- I don't see any difference in creating an embryo to use and using a spare IVF one – what's all the fuss about?

FURTHER RESEARCH

Find out what embryo research is permitted under British law.

Applied ethics

6.14 Evaluating ethical responses to genetic engineering

In this topic you will examine how the ethical theories you have studied respond to the issues of genetic engineering.

What is the response of Natural Law?

Because this ethical philosophy is absolutist and deontological, it does not consider the consequences, or benefits, of genetic engineering. What comes under scrutiny is the action itself and whether reason shows it to be fulfilling the purpose God intended. It could be argued that any research involving the manipulation of God's creation goes against the natural order of things. Equally, since sex is naturally connected with the creation of a baby, any artificial manipulation of genetic material would not be God's purpose.

Clearly, Aquinas' Primary Precept, the preservation of life, is relevant to the use of embryos in genetic research. Because an embryo is destroyed by the removal of its stem cells, Natural Law

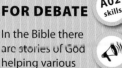

FOR DEBATE A02 skills

In the Bible there are stories of God helping various older infertile women have babies, genetic engineering is just the modern way.

One of the benefits of genetically modified crops is that they can be manipulated to thrive in the difficult climatic conditions experienced in some developing countries. It is also pointed out that the multinational companies who have patented this GM seed can charge what they like for it and have created their seed to be infertile to ensure a farmer must purchase new seed every year.

could not permit this. It could, however, be argued that an embryo is not a person, in which case its destruction is not wrong. Aquinas himself believed a foetus did not become a person until the mother felt its movements.

What do Utilitarians say?

Since Utilitarians are concerned with the consequences of an action, they would look at the benefits of genetic engineering and embryo research. The difficulty in applying this philosophy to scientific and medical procedures is that it is impossible to judge their long-term consequences.

If you apply Bentham's Hedonic Calculus to issues like embryo research, it would be necessary to consider the views of the embryo – unless you decide a five-day-old embryo has no feelings and therefore cannot suffer. Without taking the embryo's preferences into account, there are clear gains for everyone else from embryo research. That also includes money the National Health Service would save in treatments, which in turn would benefit other patients.

Utilitarianism might well argue that genetic research is likely to save a greater number of lives in the future than the number of embryos destroyed.

How does Kantian ethics respond?

The response of Kantian ethicists focuses on the requirement that people be treated as ends and not as means. This has implications for the creation of embryos for use in medical research and for the destruction of embryos regarded as unwanted after IVF treatment.

Another Kantian requirement of an ethical decision was that it could be universalised. This would be extremely hard to rule on in the case of using embryos for research because if it is said that tissue can be created for research then that must mean all tissue is to be created for research.

What is the Christian response?

The criteria Christians would employ when considering genetic engineering are to do with how much they respect the sanctity of life. Because the sanctity of life applies to humans exclusively, many Christians are prepared to accept the genetic modification of plants and, to some extent, animals. This would be particularly true where scientific advances benefit the lives of people as a result.

Because Christians believe God is the creator of life and humans are made in his image, Catholic Christians do not accept genetic engineering in the creation of life. That interferes with God's role and that of the human parents' in creating a baby. IVF is also unacceptable because it involves destroying life in the form of unwanted embryos.

Protestant Christians are more likely to accept genetic engineering, even that involving the creation and manipulation of human cells, when it is seen to be in the long-term interests of humanity.

ACTIVITY

Choose one of the ethical theories here and write their response to a couple's request for a 'designer baby'.

ACTIVITY

Read this extract from the Church of England Ethical Investment Advisory Group who:

'…recognise the potential of human embryonic stem cell research to promise new knowledge, life changing treatments and possible cures for many debilitating diseases and injuries, including Parkinson's disease, diabetes, heart disease, multiple sclerosis, burns and spinal cord injuries. However, in harvesting embryonic stem cells for research, ethical issues arise. These relate mainly to the status of the embryo and whether it has the same right to protection that is accorded to early human life, on the basis of the traditional respect for the sanctity of that life. There are also concerns over the possibility and legitimacy of "designer" babies.'

- What does the Anglican Church see as being in favour of human embryo research?
- What does it have reservations about?
- Choose another ethical response to contrast with this.

6.15 Is war ever justified?

In this topic you will consider war and how war can be justified.

■ In 2003, the prospect of Britain going to war produced an unprecedented display of feeling from the British public, as shown by this anti-war march in London. People hold strong views about this issue.

Why do people today hold such strong views about war?

War is probably the only ethical issue you are studying that has produced such a large demonstration of public feeling. That is all the more surprising when you think war is not new: throughout history people have always resorted to violence. What has changed are the methods of warfare. In the past, to most people wars were distant events taking place in far-off lands and the casualties were predominantly professional soldiers. Today, travel and communication links mean that the world has become a smaller place and we receive live battle coverage on television. The majority of casualties today are civilians, who lose their homes, their livelihood, even their lives. War spills over into terrorism which presents an even greater threat to everyday civilian life.

The development of the Just War

The issue of the legitimacy of killing or using violence against other people has occupied philosophers since ancient times. Most societies have rules that forbid killing, to prevent the community falling into anarchy, but they also distinguish between murder and killing in war or as a form of punishment. This means there has to be a clear understanding of what constitutes a war and how it should be conducted. Aristotle, for example, believed war was justified if self-defence was involved.

ACTIVITY A01+A02 Skills

- List six different reasons why a country might go to war. 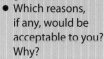 6.8
- Which reasons, if any, would be acceptable to you? Why?

Old Testament writings show the Jews believed God commanded them to fight their enemies. Stories also indicate their belief that it was acceptable to massacre non-combatants: Deuteronomy 3:24 records the total annihilation of the King Sihon's subjects: women and children included. 'We left no survivors', the scribe records.

The arrival of Jesus marked a dramatic change because he preached non-violence. 'Do not take revenge on someone who wrongs you', he told his followers (Matthew 5:39). The early Church adopted this pacifist approach until Christianity became the official religion of the Roman Empire. The Church was then required to change its approach to warfare in response to the state's political needs. St Augustine was instrumental in this departure from pacifism and his ideas were developed by Aquinas. The theory of Just War, which began then, continued evolving into the twentieth century. Today much of this theory is incorporated in the United Nations Charter and the Geneva Convention.

THE REQUIREMENTS FOR A JUST WAR

AUGUSTINE stated:
- War can only be started by a recognised authority.
- There must be a just cause.

AQUINAS added:
- A war can only be fought for a just intention which he defined as 'the advancement of good, or the avoidance of evil.'

CATHOLIC BISHOPS of America developed these clauses from Aquinas in 1983:
- The claims of both sides must be evaluated before war can be started. It is called comparative justice.
- There must be a reasonable chance of success to 'prevent the irrational resort to force or hopeless resistance when the outcome of either will clearly be disproportionate or futile.' This would prevent people being killed or maimed for a hopeless cause.
- Proportionality - 'The damage to be inflicted and the costs incurred by a war must be proportionate to the good expected by taking up arms', which means it would be morally wrong to use excessive force to achieve a small gain.
- War must be the last resort after all other attempts to resolve the dispute by negotiation have failed.
- Only legitimate targets should be attacked and there should be discrimination between combatants and innocent civilians.

Jus in bello and *Jus ad bellum*

When the morality of war is considered there are two key areas of concern which the Just War theory addresses. One is whether is it right to go to war, which is known by the Latin name *Jus ad bellum*. The other is concerned with who the war is to be conducted against, known as *Jus in bello*.

ACTIVITY A01 skills

Look at the twentieth century additions to the Just War theory. How do they clarify Jus ad bellum?

FOR DEBATE A02 skills

War is never the lesser of two evils.

STRETCH & CHALLENGE A01 skills

Go through the Just War criteria and decide which are deontological and which teleological. Then analyse how closely the 2003 Iraq War followed those criteria.

ACTIVITY A01+A02 Skills

- What characteristics does terrorism share with war and how is it different?
- How would this case be judged: a woman blows herself up at a crowded bus station to draw attention to the plight of her country?

6.16 How easy is it to put the Just War criteria into practice?

In this topic you will examine the application of the Just War theory and consider how workable it might be.

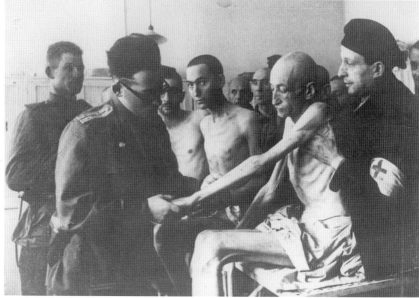

▌ The liberation of the death camp at Auschwitz in 1945 was sufficient reason for some people to say the Second World War was justified. Test that against the Just War criteria.

Let's consider the Just War theory in detail:

What is meant by a recognised authority?

It is generally accepted that only the head of the country or the state government is permitted to declare war. In recent times there has been a move in public opinion to seek a much wider permission for war. British involvement in the 2003 invasion of Iraq only went ahead after a vote in Parliament but many people wanted United Nations' authority for the war because the invasion of Iraq was not in response to an attack.

What makes a cause just?

Many would regard this as the most significant point, but equally it is one of the hardest to determine. Doesn't everybody think their cause is just? Is it possible to be objective? Augustine said: 'A just war is wont to be described as one that avenges wrongs, when a nation or state has to be punished for refusing to make amends for wrongs inflicted by its subjects, or to restore what has been seized unjustly.' In Aquinas' opinion, 'Those who are attacked, should be attacked because they deserve it on account of some fault.'

What makes an intention just?

There is some overlap here with the previous point because Aquinas defined a just intention as the advancement of good and the avoidance of evil. Here too it is difficult to be objective; most states will believe their intention is just. This point was included to prevent rulers declaring war simply because they wanted to destroy another country or for a totally unrealistic cause.

Why include comparative justice?

It was felt that if each side thought about how their opposite number viewed the situation, it might lead to a more peaceful outcome. The apportioning of punishment to the losers and rights to the winners has to be carefully balanced to respect human rights and create peace.

Is it possible to assess the likelihood of success?

It is considered wrong to start a war if you do not stand a chance of winning, because war involves the destruction of life and property.

Why proportionality?

This was included to ensure that one state does not use war as a pretext for meting out totally unreasonable force on another country. This clause is particularly important now that weapons of mass destruction like nuclear or biological warfare exist in some countries' arsenals. The harm they can cause is truly massive and must be measured against the gain. On the other hand, technological advances now make it possible to target destruction very precisely: the 'surgical strike'.

A last resort

None of the philosophers involved in the Just War theory relished the idea of war: all believed peace was preferable. This clause requires countries to make every attempt to resolve a dispute by negotiation before considering an armed response.

How realistic is it to discriminate between targets?

This clause was designed to protect innocent civilians. It requires the war to be waged against soldiers and military targets. In addition to people, buildings also have to be considered. It would be wrong to bomb a waterworks or a power station.

STRETCH & CHALLENGE · A02 skills

It has been said that because the Treaty of Versailles (which ended the First World War) did not consider comparative justice, the Second World War was inevitable. What would you conclude?

ACTIVITY · A01 skills

Invent a scenario where the response would be disproportionate. What would have been proportional?

ACTIVITY · A01 skills

- Design a leaflet for distribution amongst the armed forces. Explain the conditions for a Just War.
- Or create an ideas map that displays the conditions for a Just War. Use colour to indicate the strengths and weaknesses of each point.

FOR DEBATE · A02 skills

Negotiations are pointless. If there was a solution it would have been found long before a war was imminent.

ACTIVITY · A02 skills

Write a brief report from a military commander, explaining why she considered the central television station a legitimate target.

6.17 Is peace always right?

In this topic you will consider pacifism and examine the difference between ethical and religious reasons for this view.

What does pacifism involve?

Pacifism is the belief that war is wrong because violence is not the right solution to a dispute. Within pacifism there can be a broad range of views.

Some pacifists are absolutist and oppose the use of violence even in self-defence. As you can see from the poster, pacifism can also include opposition to activities that support war, like weapons manufacture.

Most pacifists will not undertake military service and are usually referred to as conscientious objectors. During the Second World War, when conscription came in, pacifists often undertook non-combatant duties: working as stretcher bearers or other medical work that involved saving life.

■ This poster, produced by the Religious Society of Friends (known as the Quakers) highlights the wider implications of pacifism in terms of the British trade in armaments.

There are other pacifists who take a contingent attitude to war, believing it is wrong but are prepared to accept that in some situations war may be the lesser of two evils.

Why be a pacifist?

It is possible to be pacifist for religious reasons (look back to page 167) and the Christian response is examined on the next page. But equally there are people who hold pacifist views for secular reasons and support their case with moral arguments.

(look back to page 167)

ACTIVITY A01+A02 Skills

Research and report back on a non-violent campaign of civil disobedience waged by a leading Christian, like Dr Martin Luther King or Archbishop Desmond Tutu.

Identify one situation these Christian ministers reacted to. Give a presentation on how violence was avoided and the reasons given. How effective was their response?

FOR DEBATE A02 skills

Violence is evil. There are no two ways about it!

Christian pacifism

Although we are examining the Christian case for pacifism, it is worth being aware that most religions have followers who will make a case for pacifism and Buddhism particularly is committed to non-violence.

Quakers are the only major Christian denomination wholly committed to pacifism. Their argument is that a violent response to a situation solves nothing and actually escalates the dispute. Quakers have been conscientious objectors in times of war and in times of peace are involved with the United Nations, working towards international conflict resolution.

> *Happy are those who work for peace; God will call them his children!*

Because Jesus rejected violence and preached against it in the Sermon on the Mount some members of other Christian denominations are also pacifist, and believe in following Jesus' doctrine of love and resisting violence. However, pacifism is not the traditional Christian response to war. Since the time when Augustine first outlined the concept of a Just War, Christians have accepted that war is acceptable when confronting evil.

The ethical reasons

There are secular reasons for pacifism, which this extract from the British Humanist Association's views on war and peace demonstrates.

> *Human life is all the more valuable if you do not believe in an afterlife and humanists (indeed any rational person) would think very carefully before supporting any war, because of the loss of life involved. Wars are hugely destructive, ruining lives, wasting resource, and degrading the environment …*

Evaluating pacifism

FOR

- As an absolutist philosophy it is straightforward to apply.
- It respects the sanctity of life.
- (For Christians) It closely follows Jesus' teachings.

AGAINST

- It can allow evil to flourish.
- It offers no protection for the innocent.
- It removes the right of self-defence.
- Pacifism seems powerless against modern weapons of mass destruction and mass genocide.

STRETCH & CHALLENGE
 A01 skills

Find out what a Christian realist's views on pacifism would be and produce a handout to assist the rest of the group. The views of Reinhold Niebuhr are a good place to start.

FURTHER RESEARCH
 A01 skills

Research the response of the Amish community, a Christian group in Pennsylvania, to the massacre of some of their children in October 2003. Examine the reasons they gave for their treatment of the killer's family.

ACTIVITY
 A01 skills

Read this continuation of the British Humanist Association's view on war in order to decide exactly what their position is and the reasons for it.

'Most humans are likely to say that, because we should value every human life as something unique and precious, we should look sceptically at the reasons governments give for inflicting death and destruction in war. But most humanists would also say that we have to look hard at each individual case, for just occasionally war might be the lesser evil.'

Applied ethics

6.18 Applying ethical solutions

In this topic you will consider the response of Natural Law, Kantian ethics, Utilitarianism and Christian ethics to issues of war and peace.

▌ The role of an army chaplain gives some indication of the complexity of the Christian response to war. What are these complexities?

Whilst the ethical theories we have studied all agree that human life has value and that killing is wrong, their approach to war differs.

The Kantian approach to war

As a deontological argument, Kant focused not only on the action itself but also the motivation for that action. As part of his categorical imperative, Kant required an action to be universal for it to be moral. It is difficult to formulate a maxim that will allow killing to be universal since this would go against the law of nature. Perhaps it might be possible to universalise the right to self-defence where someone is threatened by violence.

Kant's second maxim, requiring humans to be treated as ends not means, makes it difficult to justify anyone being killed in a war that is being fought for the greater good of the state. War might, however, be justified if its purpose were to liberate members of that country from an oppressive ruler.

The third maxim requires that everybody is treated as though they have the same human rights. It could be argued that this is exactly what the United Nations sets out to do.

FOR DEBATE A02 skills

If everyone followed Kant's first maxim and only fought in self-defence, world wars would end.

The Utilitarian approach to war

As a teleological theory, Utilitarianism is concerned with the outcome of war, rather than the act itself. To judge the morality of war, all the pain and injury that result from war has to be weighed against the pleasure and gain that war can produce. It is necessary to weigh up the losses and gains of both sides in the conflict. The aftermath of the Iraq War has shown that weighing up the long-term as well as immediate consequences of a war is extremely difficult.

The approach of Natural Law

The first of Aquinas' five primary precepts, the preservation of life, is relevant to a consideration of the morality of war, but it could be used by either side. War could be justified as a method of self-defence or as a way of protecting innocent lives in danger. But equally Natural Law could be used as an argument against going to war, where the loss of life is inevitable and some of that loss will be of innocent civilian life.

Others might point out that war threatens Aquinas' other primary precept, that of living in a society, since societies are always damaged by war.

Christian ethics and war

The majority of Christians believe that war is an acceptable method of defeating evil, provided the conditions for a Just War are followed. While Jesus did advocate pacifism, Christians also point to the other stories where Jesus accepted limited use of violence. Most notably, he personally violently overthrew the tables of the money-changers in the Temple in order to restore the sanctity of the place. Jesus also advised his followers to arm themselves with a sword before setting out on their ministry (Luke 22: 36–38). The teachings of the Church since Augustine have led Christians to understand they have a moral duty to fight in support of their country.

A modern Christian approach to the subject of war has been led by the philosopher Reinhold Niebuhr (1892–1971), who rejected pacifism as heresy. He argued that love cannot work in the world unless we are proactive. In an imperfect world where sin and evil surround us, it may be necessary to resort to violence to bring about peace on earth. Following on from that, he believed that a community must impose order and justice on its people – using force if necessary. The moral rules that govern the behaviour of individuals are not the same as those which govern community behaviour, since God rules through human institutions like governments and courts. Although Christian realists believe war is an evil, they accept that it may be necessary to prevent greater evils and they would accept a war which serves the national interest as morally acceptable.

ACTIVITY

Respond to a ruler who has written for advice on whether it would be ethical to invade a neighbouring country in order to rescue some tourists held hostage. You need to support your advice with at least one ethical theory.

ACTIVITY

Role-play, or script, an interview between an army chaplain and a TV show's presenter, who is a secular pacifist.

STRETCH & CHALLENGE

Investigate further Reinhold Niebuhr's claim that pacifism is heresy then explain his argument to others in the group. How might a Quaker respond to this?

ACTIVITY

Design an ideas map, or several, to display the different ethical responses to war.

ExamCafé
Relax, refresh, result!

Applied ethics: Abortion; right to a child

Debate is an important part of your Religious Studies A level. Discussions with your peers help to clarify issues in your mind. Look at the debate this group are having. What do you think?

Hot tips

Claire

I found it really hard to work out when a foetus becomes a person. The law says we can't murder a person so this issue is critical but there is no real answer: everyone says something different.

Nicole

Are there some situations where a woman should not have the right to a child? What if the woman was a criminal or a paedophile?

Helen

There are no ethical theories that really address the issue of abortion or right to a child except the Natural Law theory. Does this mean that other theories do not value human life?

Sean

Does a child with severe disabilities have the right to life? If so, what sort of life will they have? Is quality of life more important than sanctity of life? If so, why? What makes a good quality of life? Does this devalue human life to a set of material or emotional targets?

Macauly

If a child is a gift from God this must mean that some people don't deserve this gift. But what does this say about God? Why would a loving God allow a child to live in a family which abuses it, but then stop a normal couple having a child which they would love and protect?

Emma

Is it only a right because we have the technology to make it happen? Is it a good use of doctors' time and hospitals' money? Would it be better if hospitals spent money on saving lives and not artificially creating new ones for people who could actually adopt a child?

Refresh your memory

Revision checklist for Abortion; right to a child

In order to do well in this topic you will need to:

▷ Understand the concept of Sanctity of Life (life is precious, worthy of the highest respect).

▷ Understand and explain the concept of personhood and how it applies to abortion.

▷ Understand and explain the right to life as applied to abortion.

▷ Understand the rights of all those involved in abortion.

▷ Discuss the issues raised by infertility and the right to have a child.

▷ Consider whether a child is a gift or a right.

▷ Consider the status of the embryo.

▷ Apply different ethical theories to abortion and the right to a child.

Get the result!

The applied ethics questions are quite difficult to answer if you are not well prepared for them. They usually ask you to apply an ethical theory to a situation. This will mean that you must be able to explain both an ethical theory and an ethical issue. This is a test of understanding rather than just knowledge. Knowledge will get you marks but showing that you understand the theories and the issues and can relate one to the other will gain higher marks.

Read this student's answer to a question about the right to a child. Make a list of what you would change before you read what the examiner says about it. Did you spot the same problems?

Examiner says

This shows many of the misconceptions we often find in essay answers. Firstly, this candidate does not know what 'right to a child' is. Secondly, he has confused the right to a child with abortion. Thirdly, right to a child is confused with rights of a child and, lastly, Natural Law is used, but used inappropriately as this is an inaccurate summary of Natural Law theory.

Peter's answer

Everyone has a right to a child because everyone has the right to have an abortion if they don't want to have a child. However, a child does have rights and these rights need to be taken into account when deciding whether or not to have an abortion. Natural Law says that having a child is natural so we have the right to have a child. But that child also has rights and this need to be taken into account.

Peter's improved answer

Humans have the biological capacity to produce children, however, not everyone manages to successfully reproduce. Modern technology has meant that everyone has, in theory, the ability to reproduce. The question is whether having the technology means that all people have the right. Many people suggest the right should only extend to those physically able. However, many suggest that paedophiles, the mentally ill and people convicted of child cruelty should not have the right to a child. In wealthy countries IVF treatment has become commonplace and this has given more people the ability to have children. But is it right to artificially create life for the infertile rather than spend money on something like cancer treatment?

Examiner says

This is a better answer because it addresses the issue of right to a child and tries to highlight the ethical dilemmas within this issue.

Now read the following answer, decide which information is correct and which is incorrect and then rewrite the essay correcting the inaccuracies. You will also need to expand on each point that is made and try to give an example for each one. The question is asking the candidate to link the idea of sanctity of life to abortion.

Sasha's answer

Sanctity of Life means life is sacred and worthy of respect. Some ethicists suggest that this means that all life is precious and should be treated respectfully. However, this raises the questions of what counts as a life, when does life begin and what rights the unborn child actually has. It also raises the question that if the quality of a potential life is going to be poor, would it be more respectful to terminate a pregnancy. Sanctity of Life is a Roman Catholic idea and fits in with Natural Law and the Ten Commandments in that they all suggest that life must be preserved at all costs. However, some ethicists suggest that the Sanctity of Life has no place in the abortion debate as it does not allow for situations to be taken into account. This is where relativist theories such as Kantian ethics are much better.

ExamCafé

Relax, refresh, result!

Relax and prepare

Hot tips

Applied ethics: Euthanasia

Kaye

Our A' level class collected newspaper articles about euthanasia to use in our essays. This meant that we could use up to date cases to support our arguments. We could also discuss a specific case and look at all of the ethical issues surrounding that one example. We tried to apply all of the different ethical theories and religious ethics to that example as well. We are now going to try to get a doctor in to discuss these issues with us.

Callum

Once you understand the basics of euthanasia it is a straight forward topic, because it is all about our own personal rights and whether that extends to taking our own life or being assisted in doing so.

Steve

I found that the best way of discussing euthanasia is to focus on the sanctity of life Vs the quality of life. However, having specific examples to work from always helps me to learn and makes it easier to apply the ethical theories.

Maggie

I did this topic at GCSE and it is really difficult to stop myself falling back into GCSE essay mode. I have to remind myself that I need to include a lot more specific detail into my answers and explain each point I make, rather than just describing like at GCSE.

Refresh your memory

Revision checklist for euthanasia

In order to do well in this topic you will need to:

▷ Understand and explain the concept of sanctity of life and how it is applied to euthanasia.

▷ Understand and explain the concept of quality of life and how it is applied to euthanasia.

▷ Discuss the right to life as applied to euthanasia.

▷ Apply and evaluate different ethical theories to euthanasia.

Get the result !

Sample answers

Read the two answers below. Before reading the what the examiner says, decide which of the two is the better answer. Then read the examiner's comments and try to re-write these essays so that you could get full marks.

Exam Question:

'Natural Law does not provide the best approach to euthanasia.' Discuss. (10 marks)

Gursharon's answer

Examiner says

Gursharon's answer presents a good argument suggesting that Natural Law is a good ethical theory. She uses two of the primary precepts to support her argument. However, she could have explained how these precepts can be used to determine secondary precepts.

Many have suggested that Natural Law provides a clear ethical approach to medical ethics issues such as euthanasia. Aquinas' ideas stem from his belief in the sanctity of life, which alone would suggest that euthanasia is wrong. It might also be argued that primary precepts such as preservation of the innocent and the continuation of the species which are important moral principles to up hold also go against euthanasia. With regard to euthanasia these precepts would suggest that innocent life should be protected and not taken. This would suggest that euthanasia is wrong. Similarly the continuation of the species would also suggest that euthanasia is wrong.

However, the primary precepts from Natural Law do not take into account the situation or circumstances involved in euthanasia and therefore many have suggested that it is not an ethical theory which has validity. Some may therefore suggest that a more relativist ethical theory may be more appropriate. Quality of life might therefore be a more appropriate ethical principle. Others suggest, in defence of Natural Law, that the secondary precepts can be more relatively applied to take into account situation and circumstance, which suggests that Natural Law might be the best approach to euthanasia after all.

Wayne's answer

Natural Law is not the best approach to euthanasia because it does not provide an ethical approach which takes into account the situation a terminally ill patient may find themselves in. This is because Natural Law is an absolutist ethical theory and therefore laws such as preservation of the innocent would suggest that no innocent life can be taken in any situation. This goes against the idea of euthanasia.

However, if for example, someone has terminal cancer they may face a long, slow and agonising death. In this situation they may not wish to continue living. Their relatives may also not want them to go through this illness and so euthanasia would seem to them to be the most compassionate course of action. An ethical theory such as utilitarianism may therefore be a good ethical theory to use.

Examiner says

Wayne's answer is different from Gusharon's in that proposing that Natural Law does not provide the best approach to euthanasia. Despite this different approach, Wayne's answer is still a good one because he uses an example to support his point of view. If Gusharon's and Wayne's ideas were combined they would produce a much better answer. Wayne is interpreting Natural Law as an absolutist theory of ethics. He would be advised to look at page 119 for another interpretation.

ExamCafé
Relax, refresh, result!

Relax and prepare

Applied ethics: Genetic engineering

Monica

I found this topic quite difficult because it contained a lot of science and I did not really understand how cloning worked.

Michaela

I really enjoyed this topic because I can see what we are talking about when I go to my uncle's farm or watch the news or read a newspaper. This is a very real topic and not old-fashioned, like some of the theories.

Callum

I would really like to invent a time machine so I could get Kant, Mill, Bentham, Aquinas and the rest to discuss these issues. I think that they would find it difficult to apply their own theories to the modern world because so much has changed.

Sarah

I found it really useful to find out about a range of different forms of genetic engineering. I read some specific cases that have been in the news; this gives me something to hang all the ethical theories from.

Refresh your memory

Revision checklist for Genetic engineering

In order to do well in this topic you will need to:

▷ Understand and explain the ethical questions raised by the different types of genetic engineering to humans, animals and plants. So think about cloning humans, or changing the genetic structure of plants to make them disease resistant.

▷ Apply and explain the different approaches of the ethical theories to genetic engineering. Now try to work out what ethical theories such as Utilitarianism or Natural Law might say about these issues.

Get the result!

Sample answers

Exam question

b) To what extent is Kant's ethical theory a good approach to genetic engineering? (10 marks)

Tom's original answer

Kant would not be able to apply his ideas to genetic engineering because treating a soya bean as an end in itself rather than a means to an end is absurd. Kant's ethical theory can, however, be applied to humans and as long as it could be universalised (not treat people as a means to an end and think like a law maker in the kingdom of ends) we should be able to genetically engineer all newborn children to have green eyes.

If we try to universalise genetic engineering then we will end up suggesting that only plants and animals can be modified because there is no issue of personhood attached to them, so we would not need to worry about treating them as an end in themselves. Deep ecologists may disagree with this view but that is another essay in itself.

Tom's improved answer

It would be very difficult to universalise any kind of maxim to cover genetic engineering. It is too vast a topic to cover with one general law, unless you suggest that it is all morally wrong! This is where Kant's ethical theory has a real problem because it would need to produce a different maxim for each individual situation. For example: human cloning could not be treated in the same way as animal cloning and genetically modifying crops is hardly the same as designer babies, although the technology is similar.

Also Kant's ideas cannot be applied to animals and plants because we constantly use plants and animals as a means to an end and we would have to live off windfall fruit if we didn't.

This is therefore not a good theory to use as it is too inflexible and the basic concept cannot be applied. I would suggest a more relativist approach such as Utilitarianism, which would look at the benefits genetically modified crops or animals could bring, especially to places like Africa.

Examiner's tips

Find out about one issue connected with human genetic engineering, for example cloning or designer babies. One type of animal genetic engineering could be cloning again! This would give a good contrast in ideas with human cloning but would not limit your understanding of the topic. And lastly, one type of plant genetic engineering. You could choose the development of genetically modified soya beans or oil seed rape, perhaps. It is very important that you know arguments for and against each of these topics.

Search for information on the internet. Be careful though – web sites can be biased. A company producing GM crops would be biased in favour of their product whereas a group campaigning against GM crops will present the worst case possible. Therefore, you will need to read carefully the information you get.

Examiner says

Tom's is a good but superficial answer which does not really go into much detail. He does make good use of specific parts of Kant's ethical theory; however he does not give examples to support the use of the formulations of the categorical imperative.

Where do you think Tom has improved his answer? What could you do to make it even better?

Exam Café

Relax, refresh, result!

Relax and prepare

Applied ethics: War and peace

Chris

This is another of those GCSE topics which has caught me out in the past. I needed to remember to think A level and not GCSE when answering the question.

Dominic

At last, a boys' topic! It has been good looking at the ethics of war. It has given me a chance to really look hard at the fundamental elements of all ethical theories, this is how we should treat each other. It has been really interesting trying to justify killing another person and using all the arguments from abortion and euthanasia, Kant and Bentham, etc. It seems that when it comes to war some people's opinions really change and although murder is wrong, in war time the same action is praised and almost deified.

Arjan

This topic has so much to it, it is difficult to know where to start and where to finish. My teacher did lots of discussion work on this topic and this helped me to pick out which areas I needed to concentrate on and how much detail I needed to go into.

Refresh your memory

Revision checklist for war and peace

In order to do well in this topic you will need to:

▷ Understand the principles of Just War and its application.

▷ Understand and explain the theories of ethical and religious pacifism.

▷ Apply the different approaches of the ethical theories and religious ethics to war and peace.

Get the result!

Sample answers

Exam question

(a) Explain how religious ethics might be applied to issues of war and peace. (25 marks)

Extract from Stevie's answer

Christian ethics can be seen to come directly from the Bible. If they do then the Bible presents different and contradictory views on this topic. In the Old Testament there seems to be a lot of references to war, for example 'the lord is a warrior' Exodus 15:3 and 'beat your ploughshares into swords' Joel 3:9. This could suggest that as God can be seen to be promoting war then Christian ethics might also be in favour of war.

However, the Ten Commandments say that you should not murder (Exodus 20:13), which could be seen to oppose the idea of war. In the New Testament, Jesus says that we should love our enemies and pray for those who persecute us. This seems to totally contradict the Old Testament writings and present a pacifist approach.

Ethical theories linked to Christianity such as Natural Law and Situation Ethics also give different views. St Thomas Aquinas developed the Natural Law theory. The primary precepts from this theory illustrate the importance of self preservation and preservation of the innocent. This supports Jesus' ideas and would suggest war goes against what God intended for humans, i.e. reason would not see war as the purpose of human life. However, Situation Ethics could justify almost anything as it holds that love should dictate one's actions and it is possible that someone would think it OK to argue that the most loving thing for the German people in the 1930s was to kill millions of Jews and re-arm Germany.

Examiner says

Stevie could have chosen to simply describe and explain the Just War theory. However, she chose to use the Bible quotations and also for higher marks she has given some examples to illustrate how the Biblical ideas can be applied.

Examiner says

Stevie moves from these Christian Biblical and ethical theories to the Just War theory and explains each aspect of it in detail giving examples to support her answer. However, it needs mentioning that she didn't have to stick to Christianity in her answer; she could have chosen any religious tradition.

ExamCafé
Relax, refresh, result!

Relax and prepare

Religious ethics applied

Dipesh

This is a great topic because you can write about almost anything. I chose to write about Hindu ethics because I am a Hindu. However, I didn't do very well because I have never really studied my own faith in detail so I just talked about what I would do and what I have been told to do by my parents.

Fatima

Even though I am a Muslim we studied Christian ethics on our course. It was very interesting to see what other people believe. However, because we studied Christian ethics and covered the whole specification I felt confident to write about Christian ethics in the exam. What really surprised me was I felt more able to answer using the Christian ideas than my own beliefs!

Tom

I researched Buddhist ethics because I was interested in them and I used these ideas to help answer these questions. It was quite difficult to relate the theories and concepts I had learnt to practical ethics issues. I mean, when did the Buddha ever talk about genetic engineering!?

Yolanda

I found it very difficult to apply Christian ethics to practical ethics issues and I found that I needed pointers to show me what I could use and where.

Refresh your memory

Revision checklist for Religious ethics applied

In order to do well in this topic you will need to know about:
▷ The application and the different approaches of religious ethics to: abortion, the right to a child.
▷ The application and the different approaches of religious ethics to euthanasia
▷ The application and the different approaches of religious ethics to genetic engineering
▷ The application and the different approaches of religious ethics to war and peace.

Examiner's tips

Students often stay away from religious ethics initially. However, it could be a potential area of strength for candidates as there is huge scope for discussion with the ethics of any religious tradition.

Get the result!

Sample answers

Read this fairly typical answer on religious ethics applied to abortion. Make a list of what you would change and then re-write the essay including all your changes.

Examiner says

This is a good essay from one point of view because the candidate has tried to include a lot of detail from a variety of different sources in his answer. However, Peter has tried to do too much and does not really show any great detailed knowledge of the topic. This only comes from a clear explanation with evidence and examples. Peter has made a common mistake by confusing Catholic and Roman Catholic. They are the same thing.

Peter's original answer

Christians think abortion is wrong because the Bible says do not kill and this means that you can't kill an unborn child. Catholics think that you can not have an abortion in any circumstance but Roman Catholics think that you can if the abortion will save a mother's life. Other Christians think it can be okay if it is used as a last resort. Christians believe that life starts at conception and so from this point onwards you cannot kill it. Catholics think life starts when God gives it a soul which is 40 days for a boy and 80 days for a girl. Roman Catholics believe this too.

Christians also think that abortion is not natural and goes against natural law which is God's plan for the universe written into nature. We can tell what is natural by looking at it and saying that if it is natural it is okay but if it is not natural then it can not be from God and therefore it is not ethically right. Christian ethics are absolute so you must always follow their rules because they can not change at all. They apply to all people for all time and cannot reflect the situations because this would be relative and open a slippery slope to evil and hell.

Peter's improved answer

Christians believe abortion to be wrong for a number of reasons. Their beliefs come from the Bible, the church and, for some, from particular ethical theories. The Bible has been used to show that abortion is wrong by applying laws such as 'Thou shall not murder' (Exodus 20:13). A Christian might take this to mean that abortion is wrong because once an egg has been fertilised it is a life and therefore if you killed that foetus it would be seen as murder, as this is the premeditated taking of an innocent life.

Other Christians might look to ethical theories such as Natural Law. Aquinas' ethical theory suggests that there are certain primary precepts which should be followed and these can be reasoned through the use of reason. For a Christian, the primary precept which states 'continuation of the species through reproduction' would be the most persuasive. Abortion would seem to go against the idea of the continuation of the species, as the premature expulsion of a foetus would not help the species to continue.

Examiner's tips

Some suggestions to help apply religious ethics to practical issues:

- Identify what the question is asking you to write about. For example, are you being asked to evaluate how useful a religious ethic is or demonstrate the strength of using a religious ethic? You may be asked to explain how a religious ethic responds to a certain practical ethical issue or compare the responses of a religious ethic with that or a secular one.

- Identify what practical issue you are being asked about. If it is genetic engineering, remember that this is a large and varied topic and so you could focus on one aspect of it, such as genetically modifying crops, or cover the whole range of human, animal and plant genetic engineering.

- Pick a specific part of the religious ethics to use in your argument. This may help you to focus on how the religious ethic is applied to the issue.

ExamCafé
Relax, refresh, result!

Relax and prepare

If aliens visited!

When you answer an explanation question on the ethics paper, it would be really helpful to imagine that you are explaining that theory to an intelligent alien! You would need to give a clear but detailed description of the key features of the theory using examples to support what you are saying. The examples will help the alien to understand what you are saying and it will serve to convince them that you do actually know what you are talking about. (Obviously not all examiners are aliens, but this is a good way to approach these types of essays!)

You could use an essay structure like the one outlined below.

Introduction

Use the wording of the question to start your introduction: this focuses you on the actual wording of the question and should stop you from writing a good answer which does not answer the question set. Then briefly explain to the reader what you intend to talk about in your essay – the key points which need to be explained are …

Main part

A small amount of background information would be a good place to start, just to set the theory into some context. You could outline where the theory comes from, its origins, who started it and so on. Don't spend to long on this though. This needs to be followed by the central idea behind the theory, clearly explained with examples to support the points made, followed by other specific elements of the theory with examples to support the explanation, and finally variations of the theory, again with examples.

Conclusion

A brief summary of the theory which answers the question set. Remember to write in the third person. So avoid saying 'I think…' instead say 'it can be argued that' or 'philosophers such as Kant have suggested that…' or 'Bentham believed that …'

Refresh your memory

Remind yourself of what you need to include in an answer to an AO1 question by reading the marking criteria below. The column on the right explains what this really means for the exam question that appears on the next page.

AO1 Mark	Criteria	What this really means
0	absent/no relevant material	Nothing of any worth or credit i.e. "Only smarties have the answer."
1–5	Almost completely ignores the question: • little relevant material • some concepts inaccurate • shows little knowledge of technical terms Communication: often unclear or disorganised.	A limited comment about Kant's ideas or confused information about another theory but with Kant's name added.
6–9	Focuses on the general topic rather than directly on the question: • knowledge limited and partially accurate • limited understanding • selection often inappropriate • limited use of technical terms Communication: some clarity and organisation.	An essay describing some of Kant's ideas in basic terms without much explanation or evidence.
10–13	Satisfactory attempt to address the question: • some accurate knowledge • appropriate understanding • some successful selection of material • some accurate use of technical terms Communication: some clarity and organisation.	An essay which shows some explanation and some evidence of knowledge and understanding of the topic in question.
14–17	A good attempt to address the question: • accurate knowledge • good understanding • good selection of material • technical terms mostly accurate Communication: generally clear and organised.	The essay answers the question set and uses enough evidence to convince the examiner that the candidate does actually know what they are talking about.
18–21	An excellent attempt to address the question showing understanding and engagement with the material: • very high level of ability to select and deploy relevant information • accurate use of technical terms Communication: answer is well constructed and organised.	The essay deploys relevant information using technical terms accurately and shows understanding and engagement with Kant's ethical ideas.

Get the result!

Look at the exam question below and the answer given to it. What mark do you think Phillip might get for his answer? Use the marking criteria given on page 185 and the examiner's comments below to help you.

Sample answers

Exam question

(a) Explain Kant's ethical theory. (25 marks)

Phillip's answer

Kant's ethical theory is based on the belief in an objective right and wrong based on reason. Kant believed that one should act in the right way because, and only because, it is the right way to act. We should not be influenced by desires or emotions. Kant believed that if we use reason and a good will we can determine the correct course of action. To help this he devised the categorical imperative. Kant believed that if one acts in the right way then the ultimate goal is summum bonum: a state where happiness and virtue are united.

Immanuel Kant (1724–1804) was a Prussian born philosopher who was concerned with reason, objectivity and whether there was knowledge not based on experience called a priori knowledge. Kant rejected both rationalists and empiricists.

Kant's belief in reason led him to suggest that we have a sense of moral 'ought' within us which directs us to act with a good will. This means that we ought to act in a good way. Kant is suggesting that firstly we are free to act and secondly we have an in built moral code which is a priori which should govern our actions rather than desire or emotion.

Kant saw this feeling of moral ought as being our duty. He believed that we should act out of duty's sake and for duty's sake alone. However, he also felt that he needed to show a way of knowing what our duty is. He therefore felt that there should be commands or imperatives which practical reason could fathom. Kant shows that there are two types of imperatives: a non moral hypothetical imperative and a moral categorical imperative. As Kant said 'all imperatives command either hypothetically or categorically'.

Examiner says

This is a confident start to this essay. Phillip has picked out some of the key features from Kantian ethics and shown that these are the ones he will explain.

Examiner says

This is a good way of showing that you know a bit more information about the philosopher concerned. A short paragraph with background info can show your knowledge, but it is not essential and if you do include it, it should not be any longer than this.

Examiner says

This is rather brief but it does show good knowledge. However, Phillip does not really explain these ideas in sufficient depth or use examples which might suggest that he does not really understand the ideas that well. Although he does make accurate use of important technical terms.

Examiner says

This is a much better paragraph, showing clear and concise knowledge and good use of technical terms and a quotation from Kant himself. Quotations are not essential but they do demonstrate a greater depth of knowledge and understanding.

Hypothetical imperatives are not moral commands, which means that they do not apply to every one. Kant believed that you only need to follow them if you are seeking some kind of goal or end. They always start with the word if. For example; if you wish to keep your girlfriend you should treat her with respect and not cheat on her. Hypothetical imperatives usually aim towards some kind of personal desire. Kant believed that these have no place in ethics.

On the other hand Categorical imperatives are ethical commands and they do not begin with if nor do they aim for some kind of personal end or goal. Kant believed that they would apply to all people because they are produced by practical reason and are objective a priori moral laws. There are three formulations of the categorical imperative.

Firstly, 'Act only according to that maxim whereby you can at the same time will that it should become a universal law.' Kant believed that a maxim directing someone to act should be universalised so that it commands all people to act but it must be universalised without contradiction or inconsistency. For example if someone borrows money they have an ethical duty to pay it back, so their maxim would be to pay back what is owed. But if you borrowed money with no intention of paying it back then your maxim is inconsistent and it is not applied universally.

Secondly 'treat humanity never solely as a means but always as an end'. Kant believed that humans should not be treated as a means to an end. This means that you could not use some one to get a new friend or to get into a new group because this is not treating them as an end in themselves. Humans have to be treated with equal value or ethical commands will not be applied with any consistency.

Lastly 'act as if you are a lawmaker in the kingdom of ends'. Kant believed that we are all free and should remember that if we make ethical laws then we must take into account that everyone is also free to act, so our laws must apply to everyone without contradiction and treat all people as an end in themselves and not a means to an end. For Kant this demonstrates that practical reason is impartial and applies to everyone.

Kant's ethical theory is therefore based on practical reason which shows itself through having and acting out of good will. We know what to do because we have to follow our duty for duty's sake and not from an emotional point of view. To show what our duty was Kant developed the Categorical imperative to show that ethical laws should be applied to all people and all people should be treated equally as free thinking individuals.

Examiner says

This is a really good section in Phillip's answer. He has shown a very good grasp of the topic. He has used quotations to demonstrate his knowledge and backed each point up with evidence and examples.

Examiner says

This is a good conclusion it summarises the whole of Kant's argument and finishes off the essay well. If you look at the mark scheme you could get a good idea of where Phillip's answer might be placed. There is a lot of high level information here. Phillip has shown that he understands and can use technical terms. This answer is likely to get a high grade.

Glossary

Absolute means a truth which never varies.

Absolutist: a rule that is true in all situations.

Actuality is when an object fulfils its potential and becomes something else.

Analytic: a statement that is true by definition. No evidence is needed.

Apparent Good: a faulty judgement as a result of the misuse of reason or misunderstanding of Divine Law.

A priori knowledge is knowledge gained from logical reasoning, wholly independent of sense experience.

Autonomy: independence or freedom, as of the will or one's actions.

Categorical imperative: an absolute and universal sense of moral duty which directs humans to the right actions.

Contingent: dependent on something else for its being.

Cloning: a form of genetic engineering that produces a new life that is a genetic copy of its parent.

Creationism: an acceptance of the Genesis account of the creation of the universe as factual truth.

Deontological: refers to an action that is inherently right or wrong. No account is taken of circumstances or outcome.

A **descriptive statement** simply states how things are.

Efficient cause: Aristotle used this to explain how something happens, the agent which brings something about.

Ego: the conscious self, the personality that the outside world sees.

Empirical knowledge is knowledge gained from the senses.

Eudaimonia: a Greek word that means happiness through living well.

Final cause: Aristotle used this to mean the purpose of something.

Five Primary Precepts: the five basic principles of Aquinas' Natural Law.

Hedonic Calculus: Bentham's method of measuring the good and bad effects of an action.

Heteronomy: the condition of being subject to a law or standard external to itself.

Higher pleasures: those that involve the intellect like reading, art or music. According to Mill, higher pleasures are more valuable than lower pleasures because only a human can appreciate them.

Hypothetical imperative: in Kant's ethical system, a moral command that is conditional on personal motive or desire.

Immutable means unchangeable.

The **inconsistent triad** means that a perfectly good and all-knowing God cannot exist at the same time as evil.

Things continuing back forever are called **infinite regression**. Young children are brilliant at this way of thinking. 'Why is that man there?' 'He is going to cross the road.' 'Why's he crossing the road?' and whatever answer you give produces another question.

Irreducible complexity: the idea that some biological organisms are too complex to evolve without the help of an unevolved intelligence.

Lower pleasures: those that please the body, like food and sex. Because these would also please an animal, Mill rates them as lower pleasures.

Maxims: rules which are derived from the categorical imperative.

Necessary: refers to something which logically must be true.

Objective: judgements based on an impartial absolute value system.

Ontological: of or relating to essence or the nature of being.

Postulate: is something which is an initial assumption.

Potentiality: is when something contains the ingredients to become something else.

A **prescriptive statement** makes a rule about how people should behave.

Privation: means the absence, or a lack, of something.

Relativist: a judgement that depends on the circumstances; there is no universal right or wrong.

Sanctity of life: means human life is sacred.

Secondary precepts: the rules that are developed from Aquinas' Five Primary Precepts.

Subjective: judgements are based on personal opinion and not on any fixed rules.

Summum bonum is the state of supreme good when virtue and happiness come together.

Superego: the subconscious set of moral controls given us by outside influences like the rules of society.

Synthetic: a statement in which the predicate is not a necessary part of the description, e.g. 'The mermaid has a large comb.'

The Greek word **telos**: purpose. An argument concerned with the purpose, or ultimate goal, of something is called a teleological argument.

Theodicy: literally means a justification of God. It is an attempt by philosophers to reconcile the goodness and omnipotence of God with the existence of evil. Augustine and Irenaeus are two key scholars.

Theonomy: The principles and values behind both religious and ethical rules are the same.

Transgenic organism: where a living organism is given genes from a different organism like a plant, an animal, virus or bacteria.

Principle of utility: to seek always the greatest balance of good over evil.

Index